D0473610

6seconds

Self Science

The Emotional Intelligence Curriculum

Karen Stone-McCown   Joshua M. Freedman
Anabel L. Jensen, Ph.D.   Marsha C. Rideout

Second Edition, Revised and Updated

6seconds

Six Seconds, San Mateo, California

©1998 by Karen Stone-McCown, Anabel L. Jensen, Ph.D., Six Seconds

All rights reserved. Unless otherwise noted, no part of this book may be reproduced in any form, except for brief reviews, without written permission of the publisher.

ISBN 0-9629123-4-4
Library of Congress Catalog Number 98-85077

(First Edition published as *Self-Science: The Subject is Me* by Goodyear Publishing Company, Inc., Santa Monica, California, 1978 ISBN 0-87620-832-4)

Cover and book design © 1998 Joshua Freedman, Six Seconds
Unless otherwise noted, illustrations © 1995/1996 Art Parts.

Printed in the United States of America
SIX SECONDS
316 Seville Way
San Mateo, CA 94402-2853
(650) 685-9885

Most ⑥econds titles are available for quantity discount. Contact the publisher for details. (650) 685-9885

Table of Contents

Section 1: Foundations

Section 2: Developing the Group

Section 3: Developing Accountability

Section 4: Appendices

Section 3: Developing Accountability 95

Section 4: Appendices 135

Table of Experiments / Experiences

Table of Figures

Permission is granted to the owner of this book to copy the pages listed above for her or his own use.

Preface to the Second Edition

In a time when society is wracked by crisis, it is critical that we provide children tools to reach the roots of these problems; affective education is the opportunity to teach those skills to groups. At the same time, affective education is an essential tool for teachers to reach individual children.

Several months ago, Karen Stone-McCown, author of the original *Self-Science* book, suggested that now is the time to bring our affective education approaches to a larger audience. Together, we have created Six Seconds, an educational service organization to support the development of emotional intelligence through training and materials. The organization works with schools, parents, communities and organizations to develop programs to help people use emotional intelligence in daily life and as a part of education. The approach is one of integrating EQ into the structure of the school/group/family in a daily, ongoing, and comprehensive manner.

The response to Six Seconds and its resources for schools and families has been gratifying. Daily, people call, email, and fax seeking resources on how to turn emotional intelligence research into practice. In the first year of our organization we've received many requests for the *Self-Science* book — requests from all over the US, from Brazil, South Africa, Belgium, Surinam, etc. — so we decided to revise and update this incredible resource.

Since its inception, *Self-Science* has maintained a commitment to incorporating current research. While the basic framework and key elements of this curriculum remain as written in 1978, this second edition incorporates much of the emotional intelligence research since the first publication. In addition, it incorporates the expertise of an organization, Six Seconds, that has a full-time focus on teaching and learning emotional intelligence.

Self-Science teachers will also appreciate that Six Seconds is already at work on a third edition which focuses on new EQ research and teaching paradigms.

Thank you for your commitment to teaching the whole child and to making tomorrow a better place for all our children.

SELF-SCIENCE BUILDS TOOLS:

This program is unique because the activities and experiences are the **starting** point. They are the springboard that leads to learning. Self-Science is a process to teach skills and concepts — not a series of isolated activities.

Self-Science also gives teachers tools, specific techniques, and strategies. The questions and approaches in this curriculum help improve pedagogy in many other curricular areas.

From the Preface to the First Edition

If an alien were to look in on a "typical" American classroom, he might observe that the acquisition of skills that we need to succeed as human beings is left entirely to chance. He might well ask, "Where do young people learn the techniques of survival? Where do they learn how to relate to themselves and others? To communicate? To solve problems? To take responsibility for their own learning?"

For 30 years we have sought to answer those needs by creating a separate course to be taught alongside the traditional three Rs. The course is called Self-Science.

Self-Science is an affective program. Historically, affect was the private preserve of poets, novelists, and musicians. Lately, it has expanded to include psychiatrists and psychologists, who rarely enter the picture until after a child has demonstrated severe problems. It has certainly not been a concern of many schools. Education has given little systematic attention to the positive emotional development of children.

To develop this affective program, we brought together the worlds of humanistic educators with the methods and processes of modern science. The cognitive domain has been used extensively in the service of subject matter (schools often know a lot about the scientific method), but rarely in the study of self. We have explored ways to help children obtain the tools they need in order to combine the affective and cognitive processes.

As children think cognitively about affective processes, they acquire tools relevant to dealing with personal concerns. These tools fuse feeling, thinking, and doing.

This curriculum has been developed over time and through experience. It is by no means perfect, or a panacea, or meant for everyone. Any curriculum represents, at best, only one-third of a triangle. It is no more than a catalyst between student and teacher.

We believe in philosophical pluralism and realize that Self-Science may be appropriate for some schools (or even parts of some schools) and inappropriate for others. Likewise, not everyone should be a Self-Science leader. An honest self-apraisal should be your first step in implementing a Self-Science program.

In addition to the curriculum, this book includes "Notes From Karen's Journal" (with names changed in the spirit of the trust we advocate). These are offered in an effort to communicate some of the flavor and excitement of a Self-Science group in action.

SELF-SCIENCE MAKES THESE BASIC ASSUMPTIONS:

- There is no thinking without feeling and no feeling without thinking.

- The more conscious one is of what one is experiencing, the more learning is possible.

- Experiencing one's self in a conscious manner—that is, gaining self-knowledge—is an integral part of learning.

"Quick-Start" Guide

Currently there is considerable clamor to move "back to the basics." At the same time, children are faced with such incredible emotional challenges that they can only prosper with carefully honed emotional skills. It is essential for parents and educators to understand that there is no educational function more "basic" than developing affective skills. Recent research confirms that success is as much as 70-80% based on emotional intelligence. Even "objective" measures like SAT tests and IQ scores correlate directly with emotional intelligence. Clearly, for humanistic reasons as well as performance ones, it is time to incorporate emotional intelligence into your program.

In some quarters there is greater opposition to affective education than in others. Educators who perceive that they will meet with little resistance are encouraged to proceed to the next section of the handbook where information about lesson plans and teaching techniques are discussed. For those who anticipate some opposition, careful planning and positive communication with all concerned are prerequisites for a successful program. Appendix B includes several suggestions for working with colleagues and parents.

Tips for Self-Science Teachers

THE FOLLOWING PRACTICES ARE INTEGRAL TO SELF-SCIENCE:

- Express your own feelings openly, letting your likes and dislikes show.

- Label behavior clearly. Express your feelings and awknowledge patterns, but focus on naming clearly what action a child or the group has taken for good or ill. The emphasis on labeling the action but not the child is of crucial importance.

- Give feedback and reassurance. Trust grows when children feel there are no hidden surprises. The more you can let them in on what you are doing or attempting to do, the safer the group will feel.

- Experiment with several approaches, finding the discipline and group-management techniques that work best for you.

- Demonstrate good communication techniques: listen attentively, ask questions, promote dialogues (as opposed to monologues or lectures), and praise others as they demonstrate good communications skills.

- Participate in experiments and activities, taking part as a member of the group.

- Demonstrate openness and flexibility. Make it a point, for example, to choose from both sexes for partners in activities. (Sometimes boys and girls find it hard to relate in open, friendly ways. If boys tend to stick with boys and girls with girls, gently challenge this pattern.)

- Be generous with praise, using reinforcement strategies and "affirmation" techniques (see page 24).

LESSON FORMAT

Each lesson follows a similar format as outlined on page 18. Note that instructions for experiments or activities mentioned in the lessons follow each lesson. Even though the "Notes from Karen's Journal" sections follow some lessons, you may wish to read the comments they contain prior to teaching the lesson.

Scheduling Self-Science

The curriculum presented here has been designed to meet a variety of scheduling considerations. The sixty-two lessons break into two parts which may be taught consecutively as a year's course meeting twice a week or which may be divided into a two-year program meeting once each week.

Grouping Students

Since social and emotional development are roughly related to chronological age, it is best to form students into groups about the same age.

During the Open-Agenda Sessions (OASIS), for example, older students may raise topics concerning drugs, sex,drinking, etc., which are not appropriate for younger students.

You should also try to include an equal number of boys and girls in the class. Class members are more likely to feel comfortable exploring their relationships to members of the opposite sex (an important part of Self-Science learning) if they receive support from members of their own sex.

Groupings can be varied occasionally — for instance sometimes it will be valuable to meet in gender groups. It is important, however, to create enough consistency that the group can develop a shared identity.

Size

The optimum size for a class depends on the age of the students. With younger children, a group of eight to ten members is best. At that age, each child needs a chance to participate in every activity; attention spans are shorter, and children become restless if they are not actively involved.

For older students, the best group size is between ten and fifteen students. With fewer students the group becomes exclusive and doesn't provide enough variety of opinion and attitude. If the group is too large, it is difficult to establish the intimacy and group solidarity necessary for teaching the tools and skills of the curriculum.

Logistics

Logistics

MEETING PLACE AND TIME

Each lesson is planned to last approximately forty-five minutes. When lessons call for the groups working outdoors, try to schedule the class meeting so time can be extended if necessary.

The meeting place itself should be private. A sense of privacy and security allows students to open up and trust the class. Children have strong feelings about being overheard or interrupted, and the class will progress much more smoothly if the aforementioned conditions can be met. Do not, for example, attempt to hold a Self-Science class within an open classroom. Bear in mind the fact, for example, that some of the activities require shouting. While our school society generally does not encourage loud behavior, it is worth the effort to find a room that will permit this valuable Self-Science experience.

ALTERNATIVES FOR CLASSROOM TEACHERS

Classroom teachers will need to use their imaginations in order to create circumstances suited to the curriculum. Most of the exercises can be performed by entire classes. The discussions, however, are most meaningful in smaller groups. If you are working with a large class, you may find that asking students to keep journals is a more effective means of fostering personal growth. It is important that teachers keep their expectations realistic.

Team teaching allows for flexible scheduling: while one teacher works with a larger group on math, another teacher can work with a smaller group on Self-Science. In many schools, large playground areas are vacant during parts of the day. These areas can provide a meeting place. In many schools, there are conference rooms, supply rooms, even basements. Any of these (that meet fire and safety codes) can be used as a meeting place.

EVALUATING THE RESULTS OF SELF-SCIENCE

Logistics

There are many options for evaluating student performance. While grades are the norm in many schools, they may interefere with creating real trust and group identity. Narrative reports by teachers, students, and parents can be quite useful.

If the goals of Self-Science, however, are to make each student aware of, responsible for, and involved in his or her own life and learning, then the best way to measure success is to discuss it with the child. We strongly recommend, therefore, that individual conferences be held toward the end of the program.

If specific evaluations are required, however, the following criteria may be helpful:

1. Did the learner come to know and understand the cognitive steps of the Trumpet Process (see page 12)?
2. Did the learner participate actively in the course experiences and discussions?
3. Did the learner demonstrate changes in behavior?
4. Did the learner complete outside-of-class assignments?
5. Did the learner maintain confidential information?

Based upon the above criteria, the quality of individual student performances can be assessed by the teacher. A minimal response to these criteria should be satisfactory to parents. One additional input should be considered — that of the student. Have each student write a half-page, personal evaluation on what was learned in Self-Science and append those comments to the teacher evaluations.

RECORD-KEEPING

Our experiences have revealed considerable transference from Self-Science experiences to outside situations; that is, Self-Science can result in improved classroom behavior by individuals and groups of children, more purposeful study and learning behavior, better communication skills, and greater academic achievement. It is useful to maintain anecdotal reports to document this process.

History of Self-Science

Self-Science has roots in both the cognitive and affective domains. Thirty years ago, the program grew from questions about how children change their ways of thinking, and how they develop socially and emotionally. The initial development was supported by advisors including Ralph Tyler, Head of the Behavioral Sciences Research Laboratory and Ernest R. Hilgard, Head of the Psychology Department at Stanford University

From the outset, *Self-Science* also incorporated ideas and concepts from the writings of many authors, such as Carl Jung's work about unconscious processes, archetypes and the self, and Jean Piaget's writing about developmental stages and learning processes.

In developing the program, we met with Abraham Maslow about his schema of hierarchical needs and self-actualization, and with Anna Freud about her psychoanalytic work, primarily with children. We talked with Eric Erikson about the drive for identity, and tasks of children at stages such as trust vs. mistrust, identity vs. role confusion. We studied Jerome Bruner's work and particularly appreciated the spiral curriculum he describes.

We were seeking ways to design a school for tomorrow's children, and all our advisors, including Nobel Laureate in Physics, Luis Alvarez, renowned violinist Yehudi Menuhin and 10 other major contributors to society, told us that the school needed to address children's emotional and social needs as well as their intellectual needs.

For 30 years, this curriculum was a part of the Nueva School, founded by Karen Stone-McCown in 1967. Over the years, additional research has shaped the curriculum.

Section 1
Foundations

Why Self-Science?

Today's children grow up in a world plagued by violence and despair. Daily headlines assault us with tragedy and mayhem, more and more involving children and their families. Over half of America's youth are at risk (analysis of 9th and 10th grade students, US Census, 1997). Despite decades of national efforts to alleviate these symptoms, young people are afraid of being mugged in the rest room at school; metal detectors are placed at the school doors; drive-by shootings on the freeway are news only when a celebrity is involved; half of America's high school seniors have witnessed violent crimes at school — and daily between three and six of our children are killed by abuse. And our educators struggle with few tools to effectively equip students for this climate of trauma and fear.

At the same time, the last decade has seen a burst of scientific study of emotional learning and the functioning of the brain. Work by Jensen, Damasio, Salovey and Mayer, among others, gives us more accurate insight into the processes of learning, feeling and thinking. Their work confirms the fundamental principles of Self-Science as a valuable, effective approach to building a vital set of skills and understandings.

The overwhelming response to Goleman's *Emotional Intelligence* (1995), to Oprah Winfrey's ongoing effort to raise awareness of emotional integrity, and to Mary Pipher's *Reviving Ophelia* (1994) all show that our nation and the world are eager for solutions to the social plagues facing our children.

SELF-SCIENCE AND EMOTIONAL INTELLIGENCE SKILLS LEAD TO:

- Greater esteem.
- Higher motivation, creativity & achievement.
- Less violence.
- More accountability.
- Stronger classroom and school communities.

SELF-SCIENCE IS NOT

It is also important to know what Self-Science is not. It is not a program to remediate dysfunctional social skills, nor to recover from addiction, nor is it counseling. Rather, it teaches skills and concepts that support such programs. Self-Science can not replace other kinds of counseling, drug, and violence prevention programs. Instead, it works in parallel to lay the groundwork which can make those programs more successful.

Outcomes

The value of Self-Science has been proven in practice and in research. Goleman calls this program "a model for the teaching of emotional intelligence" (1995, p. 268) and devotes an entire chapter of *Emotional Intelligence* to this curriculum.

Self-Science is designed to build emotional intelligence and to develop a learning community which fosters respect, responsibility and resiliency.

The program teaches fundamental skills:

- Recognize, understand, communicate, and manage feelings.
- Recognize and redirect patterns of behavior.
- Set goals and move toward them.
- Increase respectful communication, thinking, and behaviors.

Emotional intelligence is a way of understanding and shaping how we think, feel, and act. Research suggests it shapes as much as 70-80% of "success." Certainly it is essential to interpersonal and intrapersonal relationships at school, at home, and at work. People are guided by a system of understandings, skills, and patterns. This system develops in conjunction with other aspects of personality and intelligence. Damasio, for example, writes that emotions are "enmeshed in the neural networks of reason" (Descartes' Error, 1994). This interconnected system of reason and feeling has great influence on both day-to-day behaviors and long-term growth.

Emotional intelligence includes six fundamental components, each of which have numerous sub-components.

1. Build empathy & optimism

2. Control yourself & delay gratification

3. Manage feelings

4. Socialize effectively

5. Motivate yourself

6. Commit to noble goals

These fundamentals lead to certain behaviors. Because it is nearly impossible to see what happens inside a learner's brain, educators compromise and observe a learner's behavior. While there are some serious flaws in this approach — for instance, learners demonstrate understanding in many ways — it remains a useful "yardstick" for assessment. Conversely, by learning to do these behaviors well, people develop an internalized understanding — they create new habits of mind and body. It is quite useful, then, to recognize behaviors that mark the developing EQ. Some of these are:

- Talk about feelings & needs

- Listen, share, comfort

- Grow from conflict & adversity

- Prioritize and then set goals

- Include others

- Make conscious decisions

- Give time and resources to the larger community

KNOW, CHOOSE, GIVE

Since the EQ fundamentals and resultant behaviors interconnect and overlap, it may be helpful to categorize emotional intelligence in a more general way. Six Seconds uses a three-part approach: Know Yourself, Choose Yourself, and Give Yourself.

"Know Yourself" includes naming and communicating emotions, understanding the way emotion and cognition interrelate (i.e., emotional thinking and cognitive thinking affect one another), recognizing your own patterns, and identifying your needs.

"Choose Yourself" is defined by reshaping those patterns, setting priorities, and making choices based on conscious processes.

"Give Yourself" is the aspect of emotional intelligence which concerns a commitment to the larger world — like recognizing interdependence and committing to noble goals (e.g., service learning).

Importance of an Emotional Intelligence Curriculum

Our society is faced with nearly overwhelming problems of poverty, violence, racism, and selfishness. In order to grow and survive as a culture, our children have to learn to reach their full human potential. They need to be equipped with tools to grow strong despite the negativity that surrounds them. They need strategies to manage themselves and to reshape their society.

In addition, improved EQ skills have benefits for both students and teachers. For students, these skills create higher achievement and improved social skills (Ornstein, 1986; Lakoff, 1980). For teachers, improved EQ skills increase "on task" behaviors (Rosenfield, 1990, 1991) and reduce discipline problems (Doyle, 1986).

Schools can not replace family, church, or other cultural systems that historically have shaped the integrity and morality of children. Given the current situation, however, schools do need to help reinforce those principles that we share as a society. In fact, the U.S. is the only country on the entire planet that does not have either a religious context for instruction or a values program as a framework/foundation (Hayes and Chalker, 1998). So, although it may not be appropriate for all schools to teach a particular set of values, it is essential that schools support the learning of parental and community values and the universal principles of our society.

Theory of Self-Knowledge

The Self-Science curriculum is based on some very simple assumptions:

- The more conscious one is of experiencing, the greater the potential for self-knowledge.
- The more self-knowledge one gains, the more likely it is that one can respond positively to one's self and others.

These assumptions are based upon a careful and critical study of respected research in the area of affective education. Eclectic in origin, Self-Science draws principally from Maslow's hierarchy of needs; Kelly's psychology of personal constructs; child personality and development studies; Gestalt theory; role playing; and scientific methods of inquiry.

Affective education isn't new. However, there has been resistance to affective programs in some educational circles. One reason for this resistance in recent times has been the difficulty of measuring the results of such a program. Still, even a brief consideration of current social issues and upheavals reveals that we are not totally successful in the areas of self-knowledge and interpersonal relationships. Another obstacle has been our failure to provide adequate training, funding, time, and space to this domain.

Lawrence Kubie said, "Education without self-knowledge can never mean wisdom and maturity; but self-knowledge in depth is a process, like education itself, and is never finished.... It is relative and not absolute." Likewise, Jung wrote that the exclu-

Figure 1: The Confluent Model.

All aspects of development are interconnected. Likewise, all parts of the brain are deeply interconnected. The result: thoughts, feelings, and actions are inexorably linked and must be balanced.

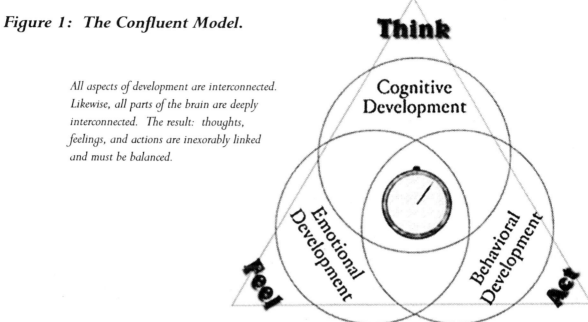

In terms of curriculum, by beginning with this confluent model, it is possible to create curriculum that leads to meaningful growth in all parts of a learner. The goal of curriculum shifts from meeting the institutional needs (completing a syllabus) to meeting the learner's needs (creating competency and connectedness). In the end, this model meets the institutional needs more effectively because learning is internalized and the learner is engaged.

sive aim of education should not be "to stuff the children's heads with knowledge, but rather to make them real men and women."

The goal, then, is to educate the whole being. Recent research confirms this fundamental truth. It is now clear that cognitive mastery only comes hand-in-hand with mastery of emotional intelligence. Life-long learning requires the use of our full intellectual prowess; the confluence of all our instinct, cognition, reasoning, and feeling. Feelings and actions are as important in determining our self-esteem, our efficacy, our very selves as is our intellectual development.

The school, as a major socializing institution of childhood, plays a significant role in determining self-concept. The give-and-take associations of contemporaries natural to that environment help develop self-esteem. A challenge to education is to define components that help children see themselves as valued and successful people.

According to Coopersmith, self-esteem is enhanced through democratic practices. He describes these practices as "freedom within established limits, encouraging the right to participate in ongoing dialogue within those limits and without penalty" (1967). Limits, he says, should be well defined and enforced, but not harsh or unduly restrictive. If limits are reasonable, children will internalize a set of definite values and attainable standards. "Without limits to gauge attainment, and (in the case of children) without the resource to form standards of their own, it is difficult, if not impossible, to gauge personal competence and success." This structure of support and of limits are integral to the *Self-Science* curriculum.

Many studies from child-development research suggest that a child's self-concept is not innate; nor is it totally fixed by the magical age of five or six. Consequently, the school holds tremendous potential for either enhancing or diminishing a child's sense of worth. This grave responsibility has been too long ignored in education. If children hear from teachers and peers six hours each day that they are "stupid," "clumsy," "mean," "smart," "thoughtful," etc., their behavior will rise or fall according to these expectations.

Clearly, then, the indispensable basis of self-education is self-knowledge. Self-knowledge is gained partly from a critical survey and judgment of personal actions and partly from support and criticism from others. Appreciation of self and recognition of the importance of self-esteem are precisely what permit people to perceive the gifts of the heart.

"Self-knowledge is not all there is to wisdom. It is an essential ingredient which makes maturity possible. Yet, it is the one ingredient which is totally neglected" (Kubie, 1968).

Structure, Scope and Sequence

In Self-Science, non-judgmental acceptance and respect of others is central to the process of personal growth. Indeed, it is central to simply hearing and seeing accurately, and thus, learning. So each lesson usually contains a focusing activity or experiment which builds trust and a sense of the group working together.

Ideally, two teachers work as a team in a Self-Science class. Team-teaching is helpful for noticing what is happening in the group, for balancing each other, and for debriefing afterwards, discussing what worked and what did not work and anticipating future objectives. Having two teachers also allows one teacher to keep track of issues and take notes to which the group might later refer. Teaming is vital when a person is a novice.

The size of the group is an important factor in determining whether or not each student learns experientially. Small groups ensure the opportunity for each individual to be actively involved. The optimum class size is 12-15 students. Group awareness and self-awareness reinforce each other; by sharing ideas and generating choices, the group becomes a unit of support for learning and a place for creative solutions. Class sessions last about 30 to 60 minutes depending on the age and developmental needs of the group.

Student Driven Content

In *Self-Science*, the **content** is wide open and is determined by children's real-life circumstances, issues, concerns, and interests. Self-Science class is always stimulating and exciting because no two sessions are ever the same; the material is alive since it comes from the participants.

The commitment to student-driven content is reflected in the structure of the lessons. Classes usually begin with a rating scale: "On a scale from one to ten (where ten is wonderful), how are you feeling today?" or "What color are you, what animal, which car are you today?" By doing this, the teacher gains a sense of the mood of the group, and can respond to their tone.

Inevitably, when a student responds strongly to the rating scale, a classmate will ask why s/he is feeling that way, and the discussion is off and running. A student might say, "I'm a 10 because today's my birthday," and the teacher might go on to ask about birthdays as symbols or about the importance of celebration. In addition, the intense social interactions of childhood are fraught with conflicts large and small — it is never difficult to find issues to discuss.

If students are very excited, perhaps because they just had a big test, they may need a more active experience so they can let off steam. Too much dialogue wouldn't work well when they are "wired." If a trauma has occurred in a child's life, such as a death in the family, a suitable activity would be a quieter, more sensitive one.

While the students supply the fuel for discussion, the teacher supplies the structure and the long-term direction. This is a cyclical, developmental process with clear objectives. (Refer to Figures 4a and 4b, pages 16 and 17, and to Figure 5, page 19). Self-Science teachers have several activities "up their sleeves" at any given time so they can respond to the group. They use these activities to generate group and individual thinking, but the activities themselves are not the focus of the class.

One of the biggest challenges of teaching Self-Science is to avoid the tendencies to take control, to wield authority, or to moralize, which some teachers have been conditioned to do in classrooms. Self-Science teachers still need to maintain order and set limits, but actually act as facilitators. They lead and demonstrate how to negotiate, they co-engage in the Self-Science process rather than acting as a manager who controls and directs from above. Finally, as the group develops and internalizes the Self-Science process, the teacher gives over more of the initiative and direction to the students.

Self-Science Culture

Establishing an appropriate culture is one of the most important elements of a successful program. The result will be a "Self-Science-friendly" environment and an invaluable curriculum.

Self-Science uses process-oriented, experiential methods such as activities or role-playing rather than content-oriented methods such as teacher presentations, textbook readings, and answering factual questions. Self-Science values the synergy and learning that comes from the interactions of a whole group rather than individuals working or learning alone or in response to the teacher. Self-Science recognizes that mistakes are an opportunity for learning versus an opportunity for judging, criticizing, and blaming.

In Self-Science, teaching is asking rather than telling; teachers encourage curiosity, exploration, re-definition, reframing, questioning, and multiple solutions rather than one right answer.

Self-Science is an experience-based program designed to equip children with emotional and cognitive skills that can broaden their understanding and functioning in all learning and social situations. Students are taught to learn and to use scientific inquiry methods in studying themselves. Special attention is given to helping students discover their own best learning styles and study habits. Outside assignments provide students with opportunities to apply their Self-Science learning as they grow.

Structure

While the authors have used the curriculum extensively in first through eighth grades, the approach has also been used around the world at all grade levels. This edition is directed to elementary school.

The curriculum was field-tested at The Nueva School in Hillsborough, California. While Dr. Jensen was Executive Director there (1984-1997), Self-Science was in place as a required, regular course from first through eighth grades.

Self-Science may also be offered as an elective or included as a mini-course within other curriculum areas such as language arts, social studies, or health. The 54 lesson course in this book may be taught over one school year (two lessons each week) or over two school years (one lesson each week). Ideally, an entire school will commit to Self-Science for a multi-year process (see Conditions for Success, page 27).

The program consists of 54 lessons grouped under ten goals. (See figures 4a and 4b, Goal Guidelines, pages 16 and 17.) The goals should be followed in sequence because the sequence itself exemplifies the inquiry process. Introductions to each goal include affective expectations, cognitive expectations, and discussions of the content and of group processes pertaining to that goal.

Building Trust

A trusting atmosphere in which students feel safe to identify their concerns about themselves and others is essential. Children sometimes need alternative affective experiences in order to realize their concerns, particularly when they are working in a group. Experiments help to evoke concerns and to unite the members of the class through common topics.

The term "approaching" (e.g., "Approaching Goal 1"), which is used throughout, is meant to convey to Self-Science teachers the idea that process learning is very much like seed planting. There may or may not be immediate evidence that learning is taking place, yet one can be confident, based on innumerable reports from teachers and students involved in humanistic education, that some growth is occurring. Accepting the idea of delayed reaction can help Self-Science teachers set realistic expectations and feel more comfortable with their role in the program. Evaluation techniques are provided periodically and their implications discussed.

Getting Help

Teachers, child-care providers, and others who work with children are always dealing with complex emotional issues. They frequently have to seek help from professionals. Likewise, remember that Self-Science is not group counseling. There are countless issues that come up in Self-Science which can be addressed then and there. At the same time, there are situations and issues that are beyond the facilitators' purview, so facilitators should feel comfortable getting help.

When setting ground rules (see page 25), it is imperative that children understand your legal and moral obligations for reporting abuse and endangerment. For less serious issues that are still beyond your purview, speak with the child first. Give him/her as much control and choice as possible — even if it is as simple as, "Would you prefer to talk to your parent(s) or should I?"

The Self-Science Process

We learn from our experiences and become more aware — yet at the same time we become wrapped-up in patterns and habits that prevent us from further learning. The first challenge, then, is to help children look at themselves without judgment and defensiveness so they can **see** those patterns. The second, perhaps greater challenge, is to support their confidence, esteem, and commitment to **change** those patterns when appropriate.

Thus, two ingredients are essential. The first is a careful observation, a scientific study of self. The second is an environment that is both non-judgmental and supportive on the one hand and committed to individual growth and accountability on the other.

Self-Science addresses both these needs. It includes curriculum to refine the cognitive process — that scientific study of self. In addition, there are approaches and activities to build community and support the development of a truly nurturing environment.

Through the Self-Science process, students learn the inter-relationships between thinking, feeling, and acting (see Figure 1, page 5). It is essential for students to recognize that they have choice about their thoughts, feelings, and actions. **Generally, it is hardest for them to accept that they have choice about how they feel.** Only from this understanding, though, can they learn real accountability. Once we accept our own power to create change, we are then confronted with our own responsibility for what actions we take and for the consequences that follow.

This level of accountability is hard to learn. It is integrity. It is acting in accord with our true beliefs. The challenge is for students — and facilitators — to move away from intentions and instead see the consequences of their choices on themselves and on others. Then, it is possible to see the impulse "beneath" the action — to see the emotional need that led to the behavior. From this, the opportunity arises to change behavior.

One principle that helps with this tranisition is that **we can not change other people.** Even when it isn't fair, even when they are "wrong." But we can change our perceptions, we can change our feelings, and we can change our responses. We can also choose to not change.

Good Intentions?

A colleague shared this story about being judgmental.

"I was working with another teacher, someone I have a strong professional relationship with, and she jokingly said, 'shut up' to a student. I told her that was not an appropriate choice. The thing is, I did it in a judgmental tone. My intention was positive and helpful — but I said it in a way which made it impossible for her to hear."

Self-Science Extends Classroom Practice
Figure 2

Traditional Classroom Values	Self-Science Extended Values
1. Learning about the world is the legitimate subject matter for the school.	+ Learning about one's self (thoughts, feelings, behaviors) is legitimate in school.
2. Remembering, planning and interpreting are important.	+ Experiencing the present moment, the here-and-now of students and teacher, is important.
3. Learning words and concepts for, and learning how to negotiate, the world of ideas and things is important.	+ Learning words and concepts for, and learning how to negotiate, one's emotions and actions is important.
4. Critical judgment and evaluation (and earned respect for performance) are central in the learning process.	+ Nonjudgmental acceptance and respect is central to the process of individual personal growth.
5. Talking, thinking, and reading about experiences and ideas are central in the learning process.	+ Experiencing one's self and one's surroundings is central to personally important learning.
6. Well-thought-out expression about subject matter is valued in the learning process.	+ Appropriate, non-manipulative disclosure of thoughts and feelings is valued and facilitates personal growth in self and others.

Self-Science requires an extension of traditional classroom norms. The extended norms are in no way meant to supplant the traditional; they are meant to supplement what already works.

Guidelines for Action

Self-Science is based on a model which combines both experiences and tools. Gerald Weinstein, a researcher in affective education at the University of Massachusetts, developed a theoretical approach to such a system: The Trumpet Process. With his approval and permission, this process became an integral part of the curriculum.

The Trumpet Process brings something to Self-Science that is seldom found in other affective curricula; it provides guidelines for action. As the scientific method is a process tool for making discoveries about the physical world, the Trumpet is a process tool for making discoveries about and acting on issues having to do with emotion and inner space.

Goals for the Self-Science curriculum have been outlined (see Figure 4a and 4b, pages 16 and 17). The first five goals help students work toward a group cohesiveness as well as orient them to certain skills they will need later on. The final five goals are built around teaching individual and group accountability. The Trumpet process provides the cognitive guidelines for making sense of the experiences in the lessons. Each step of the process will be presented in detail. The Self-Science teacher must have the process stored — and ready for use. The Trumpet Process offers the focal point for questions the teacher may ask to help students internalize their experiences.

The Trumpet Process
Figure 3

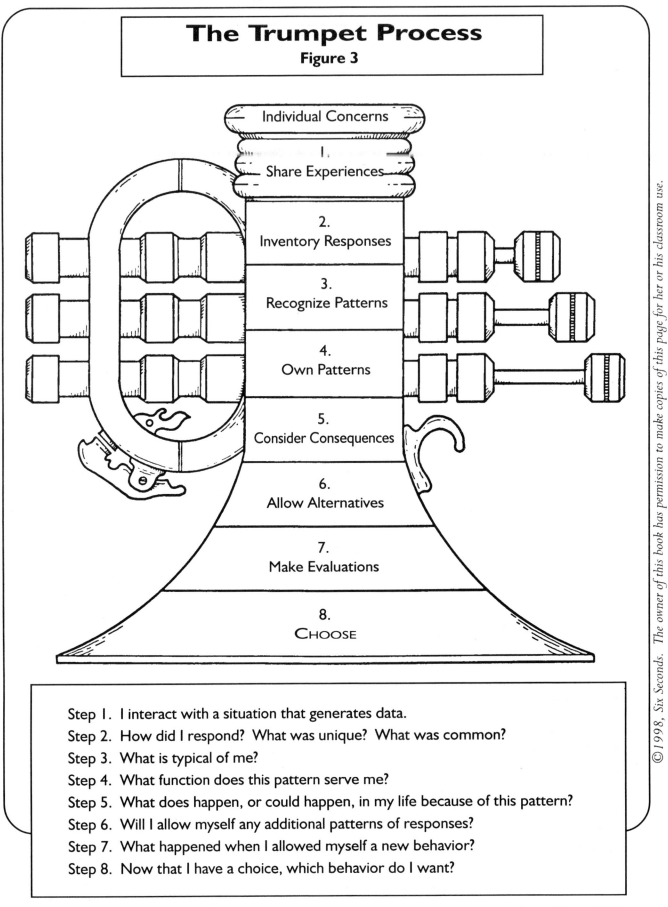

Individual Concerns

1.
Share Experiences

2.
Inventory Responses

3.
Recognize Patterns

4.
Own Patterns

5.
Consider Consequences

6.
Allow Alternatives

7.
Make Evaluations

8.
CHOOSE

Step 1. I interact with a situation that generates data.

Step 2. How did I respond? What was unique? What was common?

Step 3. What is typical of me?

Step 4. What function does this pattern serve me?

Step 5. What does happen, or could happen, in my life because of this pattern?

Step 6. Will I allow myself any additional patterns of responses?

Step 7. What happened when I allowed myself a new behavior?

Step 8. Now that I have a choice, which behavior do I want?

©1998, Six Seconds. The owner of this book has permission to make copies of this page for her or his classroom use.

Step 1. Share experiences

The child participates in various exercises or experiments that provide the class with a common reference point for discussion. Having common affective experience facilitates sharing of concerns.

Step 2. Inventory responses

The child examines and explores what happened during that experience, asking, "How did I respond? What was unique? What was common?" This stage may be the most complex part of the Trumpet Process and requires the ability to ask questions in three main areas: "What did you think? How did you feel? What did you do?"

Step 3. Recognize patterns

As the inventory process becomes more elaborate, patterns of unique student behavior emerge and are evident in thought, feeling, and action. All people exhibit behavior patterns; but most people need help in identifying and understanding their patterns. Learning about one's patterns is difficult. Most children need to be made aware of a given pattern on at least three separate occasions before they recognize its existence. In this step, the child asks, "What is typical of me?" The teacher asks, "What are you doing right now? What did you just do? Do you usually do that?"

Step 4. Own patterns

Children examine the functioning of their own patterns, understand how a particular pattern serves them and accept that it is theirs (own it). A socially positive pattern, such as volunteering to clean the white board, is easy for the child to grasp, because the child is quickly aware of rewards. Many children however, find it difficult to discover the benefits that may accrue from a socially negative pattern, such as bullying other children. The teacher may need to help them understand that even socially negative patterns serve the possessors in some way.

Step 5. Consider consequences

The teacher encourages the child to ask, "What happens or could happen in my life because of this pattern?" The child examines the price one pays for a particular pattern. The teacher helps the child to understand what benefits come at what costs and to analyze how the rewards and consequences balance out. As all patterns have positive aspects, they also have negative aspects. Most people have at least one so-cially-positive behavior pattern and generally think only of the "good" things derived from this pattern. Nevertheless, something is given up for this pattern, a price is paid. Even cleaning the white board has some costs for the child.

The Trumpet Process

Step 6. Allow alternatives

The group supports the child in helping to search for alternative modes of responding. The teacher often asks children, "What else might you do?" They think of as many ideas as possible without evaluating them right then. Using their imaginations in this way helps children realize there is more than one approach to any situation.

Step 7. Make evaluations

"What happens when I allow myself a new behavior?" Once alternatives have been generated, the child begins evaluating them by discarding the most obviously inappropriate ideas. When only one or two alternatives remain, the child commits to trying one.

Step 8. Choose

The child asks, "Now that I have a choice, which behavior do I want to use?" Conscious choice is the most important element in this final step. Children must be aware of making decisions and must take responsibility for them. The issue is not whether people choose one alternative over another or that they supplant one pattern with another. The purpose is to expand the range of choices children have so they can learn to choose an appropriate pattern according to specific circumstances. Repeating old patterns may be appropriate in some circumstances but not in others.

Looking for Patterns

Becoming aware of and recognizing patterns of responses to various situations is one of the prerequisites to having some control over reactions and increasing self-directedness. All adults can remember situations in which they did something and then said to themselves, "Why did I do that?" These situations may arise because we do not know enough about our patterns of behavior. Often children are completely oblivious to their own patterns of behavior. For instance, when two children have a fight and are asked what happened, each responds by saying something about the other child. Seldom do they communicate high awareness of their own behavior.

Helping students become aware of their behavior patterns involves focusing on the here and now. To do so, Self-Science teachers ask deceptively simple questions like:

- What are you doing right now?

- What did you just do?

- Do you usually do that when someone else does that to you?

As students learn to answer these questions thoughtfully, they come to recognize the relationship between their thoughts, feelings, and actions. With the help of a careful facilitator, they also come to see the patterns that they follow — and they understand when it will be beneficial to break from those ruts.

When beginning to work more directly with patterns of behavior, the teacher will usually find it easiest and most constructive to focus on patterns in the class. For example, in Self-Science classes made up of primary-level students, there is often a marked tendency for boys to sit on one side of the circle and girls on the other. The teacher might ask, "Has anyone ever noticed that we have a pattern in our seating arrangement?" At least some of the students will usually make the observation. You can then discuss the nature of patterns, the fact that we all have them, and the fact that some patterns serve us well and some do not.

As students become more aware of patterns in general, they become more willing to examine the functions and consequences of their own patterns. Initially, children often need a considerable amount of help to understand how they use patterns. Useful questions for discussion are:

- How many different patterns do you have?

- How many of us have similar patterns?

- What do you like about your patterns?

- What don't you like about your patterns?

- Can patterns be changed or expanded?

Fantasizing about various kinds of situations and possible patterns of responses helps students examine their own patterns. Role playing, simulation, or discussion can also aid them in examining their own behavior.

EXPERIMENTS SHOW PATTERNS

Every pattern has its pluses and minuses. If the teacher can model a pattern and illustrate how it serves, students can usually understand the idea more readily and become more willing to share their own patterns. Nearly all of the experiments and activities can be utilized this way once the students' confidence has been gained and they are sufficiently willing to examine their own patterns of behavior.

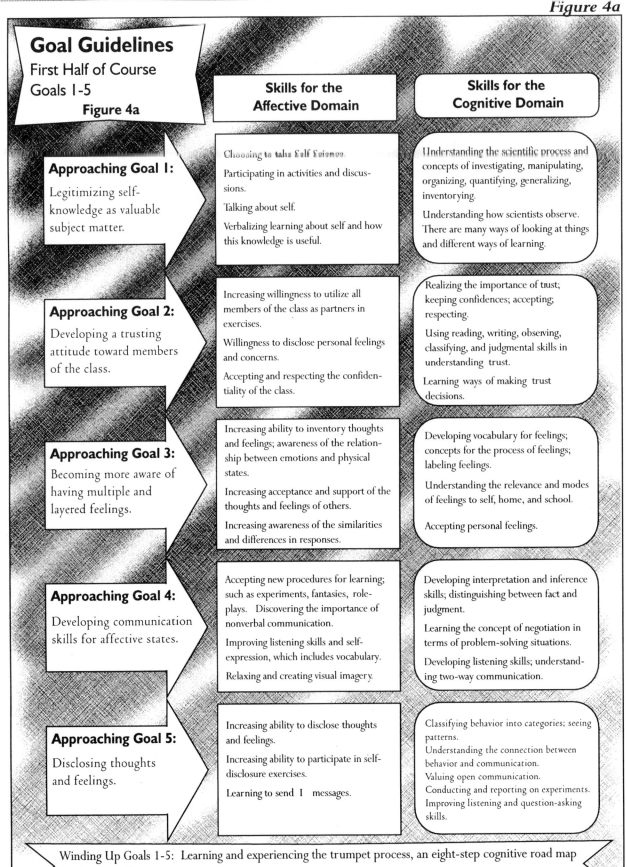

Goal Guidelines
First Half of Course
Goals 1-5
Figure 4a

| | **Skills for the Affective Domain** | **Skills for the Cognitive Domain** |

Approaching Goal 1:
Legitimizing self-knowledge as valuable subject matter.

Choosing to take Self Science.

Participating in activities and discussions.

Talking about self.

Verbalizing learning about self and how this knowledge is useful.

Understanding the scientific process and concepts of investigating, manipulating, organizing, quantifying, generalizing, inventorying.

Understanding how scientists observe. There are many ways of looking at things and different ways of learning.

Approaching Goal 2:
Developing a trusting attitude toward members of the class.

Increasing willingness to utilize all members of the class as partners in exercises.

Willingness to disclose personal feelings and concerns.

Accepting and respecting the confidentiality of the class.

Realizing the importance of trust; keeping confidences; accepting; respecting.

Using reading, writing, observing, classifying, and judgmental skills in understanding trust.

Learning ways of making trust decisions.

Approaching Goal 3:
Becoming more aware of having multiple and layered feelings.

Increasing ability to inventory thoughts and feelings; awareness of the relationship between emotions and physical states.

Increasing acceptance and support of the thoughts and feelings of others.

Increasing awareness of the similarities and differences in responses.

Developing vocabulary for feelings; concepts for the process of feelings; labeling feelings.

Understanding the relevance and modes of feelings to self, home, and school.

Accepting personal feelings.

Approaching Goal 4:
Developing communication skills for affective states.

Accepting new procedures for learning; such as experiments, fantasies, role-plays. Discovering the importance of nonverbal communication.

Improving listening skills and self-expression, which includes vocabulary.

Relaxing and creating visual imagery.

Developing interpretation and inference skills; distinguishing between fact and judgment.

Learning the concept of negotiation in terms of problem-solving situations.

Developing listening skills; understanding two-way communication.

Approaching Goal 5:
Disclosing thoughts and feelings.

Increasing ability to disclose thoughts and feelings.

Increasing ability to participate in self-disclosure exercises.

Learning to send I messages.

Classifying behavior into categories; seeing patterns.
Understanding the connection between behavior and communication.
Valuing open communication.
Conducting and reporting on experiments.
Improving listening and question-asking skills.

Winding Up Goals 1-5: Learning and experiencing the trumpet process, an eight-step cognitive road map for charting affective progress.

Figure 4b

Goal Guidelines
Second Half of Course
Goals 6-10
Figure 4b

	Skills for the Affective Domain	**Skills for the Cognitive Domain**

Approaching Goal 6:

Enhancing self-esteem in terms of awareness and acceptance of strengths.

Affective: Increasing ability to think and talk more positively about self.

Increasing ability to laugh at self.

Expressing pride in self.

Accurately describing personal strengths and weaknesses.

Cognitive: Learning to make evaluations and judgments.

Relating emotional concepts to characters in fiction, myths, and folk tales.

Reinforcing skills in classifying data.

Approaching Goal 7:

Accepting responsibility for attitudes and actions.

Affective: Increasing acceptance of personal feelings, moods, conduct, and the consequences of behavior.

Increasing the ability to follow through on commitment.

Cognitive: Understanding concepts of projection and avoidance.

Applying evaluation skills to study habits.

Approaching Goal 8:

Becoming aware of major concerns/worries/anxieties.

Affective: Increasing the ability to state specific personal wants and needs and relate personally to the wants and needs of others.

Cognitive: Integrating the skills and concepts developed thus far.

Approaching Goal 9:

Recognizing present behavioral patterns; learning about personal learning styles.

Affective: Increasing the ability to describe personal behavioral patterns.

Identifying individual learning patterns.

Increasing awareness of the consequences and functions of behavioral patterns.

Cognitive: Stating and using individual learning patterns and styles.

Application of the process tools learned thus far.

Approaching Goal 10:

Experimenting with alternative behavioral patterns; choosing optimism and hope.

Affective: Increasing the ability to conceptualize alternatives.

Increasing the ability to experiment with new behavior.

Accepting limitations.

Cognitive: Understanding the processes for making changes.

Winding Up Goals 6-10: Understanding the tools now available and sensing when the tools will be useful. Acquiring a sense of accomplishment and closure.

Lesson Structure   Each lesson in Self-Science follows a similar format and, where appropriate, includes these features:

1. Introduction to the concepts.

2. Assignment that can lead up to each lesson.

3. Materials.

4. Affective Experience—The core of each lesson is a directed experience which provides firsthand material for cognitive inquiry. The experiences include experiments, simulations, and other group activities. They make use of such inquiry techniques as brainstorming, fantasizing, and role playing.

    Self-Science uses these experiences to further the cognitive expectations stated. Each experience is followed immediately by discussion questions whose purpose is to help students learn and use such inquiry methods as identifying, observing, classifying, and noting similarities and differences.

4. Cognitive Inquiry—This portion of each lesson is devoted to comprehending and extending the reactions which developed during the experiences, usually by means of a group discussion guided by the teacher. Students develop relevant vocabulary and a grasp of central concepts during these inquiries.

5. Instructions for experiments and activities — procedures, discussion questions, follow-up activities, and frequently, variations are included.

6. Notes from Karen's Journal — This section follows many of the lesson plans. They share some of the vivid experiences encountered during several years of teaching Self-Science at The Nueva School. The extracts from journals and diaries may help you to anticipate or better understand similar experiences with your own group.

KEEP A COMPASS HANDY

The sequence is carefully structured in accordance with the spiral theory of learning; as the program advances, students work in greater depth and complexity, calling on approaches they have experienced earlier. Even though special group needs may call for the occasional detour, it is important that you return to the sequence and build the cumulative skills. In addition, a successful whole-school program will return to the fundamental skills over and over — each time students encounter the principles they can reach a greater depth and sophistication (see Figure 5, Scope and Sequence Spiral, page 19).

Figure 5: Scope and Sequence Spiral

At different stages, students need to return to key principles and refine them in a new developmental context. Expectations should reflect developmental growth; a seventh grader, for example, has a far more complex ability to self-assess than does a third grader. She may need help, though, to see the ramifications of her own development and to apply her new skills.

Open Agenda Sessions Initiated by Students (OASIS)

Unstructured lessons should be incorporated in the Self-Science sequence. Their purpose is to provide opportunity for discussion of group-initiated topics. In themselves they constitute experiences in reaching some of the expectations of Self-Science (e.g., taking responsibility for one's own learning, participating openly, and dealing with sensitive subject areas). Appendix E (see page 158) contains suggestions for OASIS along with excerpts from Karen's journal on various key topics. Once familiar with the curriculum, you will likely increase your use of OASIS.

In addition, several of the lessons in the sequence are short enough to incorporate OASIS along with a structured lesson. In any case, since content for lessons is student generated, at times facilitators will need to abandon planned lessons in favor of processing current issues.

These sessions can be similar to class meetings held in many schools. The challenge is to bring Self-Science skills like careful observation to the table when discussing

emotionally charged issues. It is essential that facilitators are firm about groundrules (see page 25) and that students accept that the purpose of open-agenda sessions is not simply to air grievances. This is an opportunity for self-study and problem solving. To facilitate that commitment, use the Trumpet Process and the inquiry-based dialogue techniques.

REFLECTION FROM A SELF-SCIENCE TEACHER: WHAT DO YOU REALLY NEED?

One day a student and teacher both came to me independently to ask for help with a conflict they were having. I made a terrible mistake facilitating because I let the student start without getting a clear commitment that we were going to attempt to find a solution.

The student was able to describe her actions and feelings, and the teacher did the same. Then, we tried to find solutions; I asked what each felt they needed or wanted to resolve the problem. The student got stuck and could not agree to try any solutions.

It turns out that what she really wanted was for the teacher to accept her bad behavior. To her, that would show he accepted her unconditionally. Clearly, she was not going to get that... and since we had not started by agreeing to find a solution, we made no progress.

Self-Science Teachers and Techniques

The main difference between teaching a traditional subject and teaching Self-Science is your role in the classroom. The traditional classroom teaching role often approaches that of a manager (i.e., the teacher is primarily concerned with controlling and directing students). In Self-Science, you must certainly maintain order and set limits, but think of yourself as a "facilitator," a person who leads and pulls and tugs and demonstrates how to negotiate and keep the process going.

Traditional curricula center around what you teach and how you teach it. In Self-Science, the focus is almost reversed. How you teach is in itself a demonstration of using the scientific method to study self. You might say that how you teach is what you are teaching in Self-Science. In such a curriculum, who you are and what you personally demonstrate is a great part of what you are teaching — the Rosenthal effect ("You get what you expect") certainly operates here.

Teaching a Self-Science class can be an exciting journey in your own development. Start by extending your own self-image and seeing yourself as a role model and group leader; these are parts of your teaching repertoire.

You Teach What You Are

A Self-Science teacher's role exceeds simply creating a safe environment. Preparing to teach Self-Science requires more self-reflection than preparing for teaching most subjects. Children learn from the style of the teacher. Who you are and what you personally demonstrate is a great part of what you are teaching.

Students are remarkably perceptive. They observe, both consciously and unconsciously, and experiment with behaviors that they see. As a facilitator, you are a part of the Self-Science group. Your honest emotionality, your care with other's emotions, your word choices, your follow-through on commitments are all integral to the child's learning. While we all make mistakes, children have little tolerance for hypocrisy — so whatever you ask of them, ask more of yourself.

The more you can let children in on what you are doing or attempting to do, the safer the group will feel. Teachers can model trust by expressing their feelings openly, labeling actions clearly but not labeling children, giving feedback and reassurance so there are no hidden surprises. Teachers build trust by participating in experiments as a member of the group.

Providing a role model is not a magical process. It simply means being yourself, while perhaps changing the emphasis on certain skills you already have. Your hardest job may be to examine the conditioning behind your own (possible) tendencies to take control, wield authority, and moralize. While you will never let go completely (this still is a classroom), your efforts should be toward working for greater initiative from the group and less direction from you as time goes on.

To help you develop your skills as a facilitator, see Appendix A. It includes a few simple exercises as well as a "script" that demonstrates taking a group through the Trumpet Process.

There are certain techniques that are extremely useful for creating affective experiences. They include dialogue, role playing, experiments, simulations, expression through art, games, and fantasy. As facilitators become more experienced and aware of the underlying process of Self-Science, they will invent, adopt, adapt, and create new activities. They will also learn to use these pedagogies with children of any age. The observations and discussions about the activity will vary depending on age and maturity of the children.

Questioning

Central to the whole process of teaching Self-Science is improving communication — helping children learn how to transmit messages effectively, to listen actively, and to ask productive questions. The opportunity to learn — to make a conscious appraisal of ideas — pivots on the cognitive inquiry process. This inquiry process integrates cognitive and emotional intelligence. Asking questions puts the focus on learning rather than teaching.

The Self-Science approach to effective questions is beginning with "what" not "why" questions. Starting with "why" questions leads to non-productive, defensive, and circular responses, whereas, "what" questions encourage precise, non-judgmental observation. This process of careful observation is the science in "Self-Science."

What do you see?

What do you hear?

What are you thinking?

What do you feel?

What just happened?

What did you just do?

What were you feeling about that?

What do you mean by ...?

What if...?

What would be the consequences of that thought, feeling, or action?

What other possibilities are there?

Would you really do that or are you just talking?

Do you do this often?

Would you do the same thing over again?

TRANSFERABLE SKILLS

One of the critical questions for every lesson is, "What is the skill we just learned?" Even more important is the follow-up: "Where else can you use this skill?"

These are the kinds of questions to use over and over. Not only will you help students sharpen their cognitive skills, but you will model appropriate and healthy modes of coping and analytical behavior.

Our second general questioning approach is to constantly use the group as a mirror for expectations and experiences. "Does anyone else in our group feel the same (differently)?" This kind of question creates awareness of self and others; builds reassurance by sharing similar thoughts and feelings; enhances self-esteem by permitting recognition of differences. There is an underlying premise of respect for the thoughts and feelings of others.

Dialogue

Since Self-Science classes have communication as one goal, children need to engage in constructive discussions in the group. Self-Science dialogue often revolves around events that arise in the lives of the children. For example, a birthday, a new sibling, a holiday, a test, the death of a pet, a fight with a friend or news story are all potential discussion topics. Discussions in Self-Science are not adult-driven; the teacher acts as a facilitator working to unfold the children's views.

Children know that their time to speak is limited, although sometimes they may forget and need to be reminded. Having a signal to tell them it's time to wind up what they are saying is helpful. Children learn to actively listen to the person who is speaking. They develop reflective, inquiry-based listening skills as modeled by the facilitators. With help, they learn to ask clarifying questions and to make comments that add depth to the discussion. Students often think about what they will say when it's their turn, or focus on the fact that their hand has been up.... so facilitators will use techniques to put attention on the speaker. Listening is often one of the most neglected communication skills.

Role-playing

Role-playing provides an opportunity to be someone or something else. They are kinesthetic metaphors. This technique is useful for exploring emotionally-laden topics, for seeing other points of view. It helps students examine alternatives and discover consequences.

When the goal is to generate self-awareness, students can play themselves or see other students playing them. The teacher might say, "Sarah, role play how you express frustration." Then to another student, "Now, you play Sarah." Sarah may see herself as assertive while others experience her as aggressive. The teacher then asks, "Do others see you as you see yourself?" When the intent is to aid the student in seeing another point of view, the teacher might cast the student in a role directly in conflict with his or her own position. Because role-playing provides grist for follow-up discussions, it is advisable to keep the period of role-play brief.

Simulations, or extended role-playing activities, can be useful in Self-Science. Since classroom teacher often use simulations, there may be opportunities to team.

Fantasy

Fantasy is a process of creating mental images; it is like role-playing within your head. The Animal Fantasy invites students to imagine that they are an animal walking in a meadow. They see another animal — their worst enemy! The facilitator then asks questions to help the student inventory, or list, their emotional responses to the situation.

Experiments

An experiment in Self-Science is an activity that includes observation of a phenomenon, data gathering, reporting results, and making conclusions. For example, children are divided into small groups and each group is given a deck of cards. The instructions are, "Build a 3-story house of cards. Pay attention to your inner dialogue and your interactions within the group." The teachers note the children's frustration levels rising as they attempt to add the third story and it falls down, over and over. The teachers stop the experiment after some negative interactions but before things get out of hand. Then the teachers help the students record and analyze data on the blackboard, "What did you notice about yourself? What did you notice about other people?" Finally, they discuss conclusions about their patterns in relation to frustration. "Is this your normal pattern? What are the consequences? What are alternative ways of responding to frustration?"

Affirmation

Affirmation is used in Self-Science to help students gain a clearer recognition and overview of their strengths, personality resources, capacities, and their potentialities. The first step is to spend a few minutes making a general list of personality strengths. The class breaks into groups of five or six. Focusing on one group member at a time, the group bombards the member with the strengths they see.

Expression Through Art

Art is another form of communication. Children fold paper, draw, make clay sculptures, or do sand paintings in Self-Science to become more aware of their feelings, to express how reality looks from their perspective, and to create a vision of future possibilities. For example, children can draw pictures of feelings they have inside and those they have outside. They talk about their excitement (outside) about dressing up for Halloween, and their fear (inside) that they might get scared and cry in the haunted house. They draw these feelings which helps them express themselves and acknowledge that they can feel more than one way at a time. The teacher asks questions to help children learn how they can align inside and outside feelings.

Student Journals

Students sharpen their powers of observation and awareness by keeping private journals, and entries are shared only if the student wishes. The journals also serve to provide a sense of progress for the student as they note increased vocabulary skills, improved problem solving skills, recognition of their patterns, and an understanding of the consequences of those patterns to themselves and others.

Ground Rules

TRUST AND PRIVACY

It is important for both children and facilitators to bring issues from Self-Science outside; everyone should be talking to parents, other teachers, and working on problems on an ongoing basis. So, the privacy rule means you can talk to others about what happened in Self-Science class and what you shared, but you may not quote other people. The only exception is if a matter of health or safety arises.

Since the discussions that come up in Self-Science are private, and building the atmosphere of trust so important, visitors are rarely allowed in the sessions. It's helpful to have a sign on the door that says, "Do not disturb," and see that it's respected by staff, students, and parents.

KILLER STATEMENTS

Not only during Self-Science but throughout school, students agree that no "killer statements" are allowed. Killer statements are verbal as well as nonverbal communications that hurt, criticize, demean or reject oneself or others. Such statements kill another person's essence. "You're stupid" is an example of a killer statement. Children learn to recognize killer statements and call one another on using them so that all are protected from negative feelings.

DIRECT CONTACT

Self-Science teachers encourage students to speak directly with the person with whom they had a conflict, issue, or any kind of incomplete communication. The child might wish the teacher's support in doing this; however, the teacher encourages the child to initiate discussion with the other individual so as to have resolution rather than an ongoing difficulty.

GROUND RULES

Ground rules are critical to Self-Science. They shape the encounters and provide a structure to manage difficult topics. Mainly they have to do with how communication takes place — the ways people in Self-Science will speak to one another. As such, they are also valuable for school in general. Children should be involved in creating ground rules; the concepts listed here should be incorporated.

I-MESSAGES

I-messages are the first step to successful communication about an emotional topic. "I feel mad when you tell me to 'shut up' — I feel like you don't respect my ideas." "I feel angry when you lie to me." "I feel sad when you leave me out." The next step is for children to state what they want, "I want you to tell me the truth." "I want you to include me." Older students can also identify and express consequences. "I felt disappointed when you didn't call me on the telephone last night as you promised. I want you to keep your agreements with me. If you don't, I will find it hard to trust you."

PASSING

Students are in charge of the level at which they participate in Self-Science. If s/he is uncomfortable with an activity or does not want to participate, s/he can say, "I pass," and watch attentively. A child absorbs a great deal simply by observing. The teacher might afterwards take the student aside and ask if anything had occurred in the class that the child needed help with understanding or wished to learn more about.

The exception is that once a child brings up an issue or voices a concern, it is not acceptable to "give up" and withdraw. It may be necessary to defer discussion or to create another venue, but children have to own their issues and own their solutions.

Before teachers and administrators consider initiating a Self-Science program, they should explore and clarify their own responses to these major questions:

- Are the goals of Self-Science consistent with my personal values?
- Are the goals of Self-Science philosophically consistent with the values of the school where I teach?
- Do teachers have the leadership qualifications for Self-Science?

Self-Science teachers need to ask themselves...

Do I appreciate children? Do I recognize and accept children's emotional and social needs; am I child-centered rather than subject-centered?

Do I have self-knowledge? Do I know enough about myself to help children learn about themselves?

Am I open? Am I able to share my feelings and thoughts; can I say, "I don't know."

Am I warm? Do I show a friendly, caring manner; am I relaxed in most situations; do I help others feel relaxed? Do children feel I like them?

How accepting am I? Do I accept myself and others; do I see feelings — mine and other people's— as valid? Do I accept the positive and negative in all of us?

Do I show support? Am I able to be an advocate for the child — even when I don't agree?

Am I flexible? Can I alter a course of action; can I flow with the mood of the class; can I respond constructively to the unexpected? Can I creatively reframe situations and put them in a new light?

Am I empathic? Do I recognize the feelings that others have? Can I identify feelings clearly?

Do I show respect? Do I listen to all points of view; do I work to overcome my biases? Do I manage my feelings so I don't blame or defend?

Am I accountable? Do I believe in natural consequences? Do I let children learn from their mistakes or do I rescue them?

Do I set and move towards goals? Do I see the big picture? Do I give myself to the larger community? Do I have hope for the future?

Conditions For Success

Self-Science Teachers Need...

Community Agreements

Teachers and administrators need two kinds of support to gain acceptance for a Self-Science curriculum within the school. First they need agreement from the administration, the other teachers, and the parent leadership that the teaching of emotional intelligence is important and valued. Second, they need to identify at least one other person on the staff who is willing to support their efforts.

It is necessary to get agreement about whether Self-Science is an elective class or a required class and whether teachers will work with a co-leader. Finally, it is necessary to determine how children will be assessed. There is a range of possibilities including a pass-fail system based on attendance and completed assignments, anecdotal reports by students and teachers about behavior changes, parents' survey response forms, children checking their own journals and assessing their own progress, or using standardized measures of self-esteem. In Appendix D, there is a sample rubric (see Figure 15, page 157) that can be used to assess emotional intelligence and the use of EQ skills.

It is difficult to imagine a situation where a Self-Science curriculum would not benefit children. If children begin to gain emotional competence at an early age, they are more likely to have fulfilling lives, to be better members of their families and communities, and better citizens of the world. We have found Self-Science to be an exciting journey for both teachers and students.

EFFECTIVE AFFECTIVE PROGRAMS

Research of effective affective programs demonstrates six key commitments that will help make your program successful:

1. Driven by student / community needs.

2. Supported through ongoing training of staff, students and parents.

3. Commitment to effective brain-based pedagogy (choice, humor, discussion, dilemmas, high-order questions, manipulatives).

4. Consistent time for small group discussion with consistent facilitator-guides.

5. Whole school/community involvement (culture of cooperation, positive conflict, celebrations, respect, responsibility, resiliency).

6. Assessment, evaluation, refinement.

Section 2
Developing the Group

The curriculum is structured in accordance with the realities of group process. The first phase of the course is a group-growing-together time, a time for learning concepts and vocabulary, and for having basic experiences which are for the most part external and which take place in a climate of safety.

The thirty-eight lessons cover nineteen weeks if you are using the two-lessons-a-week plan. This brings you to approximately the end of February, if you start in September, or to the end of the school year, if you start after the winter vacation. Using either of these plans provides a convenient stopping place before the class moves on to the second phase of the curriculum.

It is a part of our American heritage to resist being managed, and it should not surprise us if such techniques call forth in students ingenious and creative devices for sabotaging the system.

— *Arthur W. Combs,*
Humanisitc Education
Sourcebook

Approaching Goal I

Legitimizing Self-Knowledge as Valuable Subject Matter

Most children have not thought that learning about themselves is a part of school. Nor have they thought about how you learn about yourself or about what there is to learn. Lessons one through four are concerned with establishing excitement and curiosity about using scientific methods to study one's self. Themes for future meetings will be discussed during these lessons.

GROUP BEHAVIOR

At this point in the program, the group is just coming together, with some anxieties, some curiosity—perhaps even some skepticism. Only later will individuals merge into a group characterized by trust and solidarity. In this first stage, you will be helping the group discover the purpose for their meeting. You will be providing experiences meant to demonstrate that Self-Science is a place where "we study ourselves like scientists do" and "where we learn about ourselves."

EVIDENCE OF AFFECTIVE GROWTH

- Choosing to take Self-Science.
- Participating in the activities and discussions.
- Talking about one's self.
- Verbalizing what is being learned about self and how this knowledge is useful.

EVIDENCE OF COGNITIVE GROWTH

- Understanding the scientific process.
- Understanding concepts of investigating, manipulating, organizing, quantifying, generalizing, inventorying.
- Understanding how scientists observe. There are many ways of looking at things.
- Understanding different ways of learning.

Welcome the children. Introduce yourself by sharing a story about yourself that the group doesn't know. Begin the process of becoming a model for the group by sharing your emotions and being self-reflective.

Lesson I:
Set the Stage

AFFECTIVE EXPERIENCE

- Introduce the "rating scale" by asking each person to say how they feel on a scale from one to ten. Once through, invite questions or comments.

- Introduce the Bumpety-Bump Experiment (see page 34).

- Explain the rules. Play two or three times with first names.

- Play again with animal names, then with feeling words. (How the group handles feeling words is a good barometer of the group process at this point.)

- After each experiment, use the discussion questions to focus on what students are learning about themselves and each other.

COGNITIVE INQUIRY

Have the students sit quietly in a circle and proceed with the first group discussion.

1. Establish the reflective inquiry process by asking detailed questions about the experiments you just completed and how individuals felt and acted.

2. Brainstorm. "What do you think Self-Science is?" Have someone list responses on the chalkboard (e.g., activites, learning about ourselves, learning about feelings and behavior, getting to know ourselves).

3. Seriously discuss the purpose of Self-Science (see page 43).

4. Begin to establish ground rules (see page 25). Brainstorm, "what are some ground rules to help us accomplish all of these (from questions 2 and 3)?"

5. Introduce the word "inventory."

6. At closure, thank the group for coming and participating.

The Bumpety-Bump Experiment will be used often throughout the program.

Don't try to apply the discussion questions in depth at this time.

The Bumpety-Bump Experiment

This is a good introductory, warm-up, or change-of-pace activity. It is useful in eliciting "here-and-now" feelings.

Improvise questions along these lines depending upon the content of the game. Early in the program, remind everyone that they have the right to pass if they don't wish to respond.

PROCEDURE

Have the group stand (or sit) in a circle. Each participant must ask and then remember the names of the people on either side (teachers play, too). Someone is asked to volunteer to be "It." "It" stands in the center of the circle, points to someone, and says out loud, "Bumpety-bump—one, two, three."

The person pointed to must say the name of one of the people next to him/her before "It" finishes counting. If the person wins, "It" points to somebody else. If the person cannot remember the names or say them quickly enough, then s/he becomes "It."

DISCUSSION QUESTIONS

1. "What did you observe during the game?"

   (During the first few days, you may have to probe for answers, either asking for volunteers or going around the circle (e.g., "Is there any pattern in the way the 'It' people made their choices? Do boys always choose boys? Do girls always choose girls? Do some people not try because they want to be 'It'?")

   Sometimes you may want to let some children monitor the experiment by observing rather than participating, and then giving the group feedback afterwards.

2. "How does it feel when someone remembers your name?"

3. "How does it feel when someone forgets your name?"

4. "Does anyone else in our group ever feel that way?" (Children learn a great deal about themselves and others by becoming aware of the similarities and differences in their responses. This question can be asked over and over, in almost every game and subsequent discussion.)

5. "What makes you want to be a _____ (name of animal)? What would you do if you were that animal right now? How do you imagine this animal right now? How do you imagine this animal feels about him or herself? Do you ever feel this way? When?"

6. "You chose _____ for your feeling word. Do you often feel that way? What made you feel that way today?"

VARIATIONS

1. Call out first and last names.

2. Call out first name of both the people on either side.

3. Call out an animal you think is most like you today.

4. Pick a word that describes the way you are feeling right now.

5. Pick a word that describes the way you most like to feel.

6. Pick a word that describes the way you least like to feel.

7. Name something you want very much.

8. Name one good thing about yourself.

Lesson 2: Inventories

BEGINNING

Share inventories brought in as homework (see "Assignment" in the margin). Point out the kinds of things being inventoried (probably predominantly physical or behavioral). Elicit a response of how little we really know about ourselves and each other.

Sometime in this lesson, review "confidentiality" (see page 25).

AFFECTIVE EXPERIENCE

- A variation of Bumpety-Bump: ask players to "name one positive thing about yourself" (see page 34). Repeat the experiment, this time with some children monitoring (observing and noting behaviors).

- Discuss what the experiment reveals about the students. Ask, "What did we just do?" (Participate in an experiment.) "What did the experiment reveal? Did monitors see anything differently than the participants?"

- Try the Elephant and Giraffe Experiment (see page 36).

- Introduce the No Teachers Fantasy Experiment beginning with a relaxation technique (see page 36).

- Ask discussion questions concerning behavior during the experiments.

ASSIGNMENT

Make a self-inventory — a list about yourself (physical description, likes, dislikes, your birthday...). The list may be as long or as short as you want.

COGNITIVE INQUIRY

1. "What is fantasy?"
2. "What is monitoring?"
3. "What is feedback?"

Establish these techniques as ways of seeing ourselves. Develop the analogy of not being able to see yourself when you swing a baseball bat — but others can see you. Discuss self-knowledge by asking:

4. "Did you ever hear of self-knowledge?"
5. "Why isn't self-knowledge taught? Is it important? Why?"
6. "Are you an environment? How?"
7. "Where does the world around you begin?"
8. "What would you study if you could only study self? How?"
9. "How come we rarely study ourselves?"
10. "Can you see yourself learn?" (Promise you will say and do something about this question later.)

DON'T FORGET

Somewhere in each lesson, be sure to ask the group to identify the specific skills they just learned and to give ideas of where else this skill could be used.

Elephant and Giraffe Experiment

This activity is used as an introductory warm-up exercise to get people moving, thinking, and cooperating. The person who is "It" stands in the center of the circle, points to any person in the circle, and says either, "Elephant—one, two, three, four, five, six," or "Giraffe—one, two...." If you are pointed to and called "elephant," you bend from the waist and make a trunk with your arms. The people on either side of you put their hands to your head to make ears. If you are pointed to and called "giraffe," you put your arms together above your head and the people on either side of you place their hands on your waist to form legs. Whoever fails to do his/her part before the end of the count becomes "It." This is a fun, fast-paced activity that can go on as long as the participants are interested in playing.

No Teachers Fantasy Experiment

Ask the children to relax as much as possible and imagine that they are students in a classroom— their own classroom or some other classroom. "On the first day you arrive, your classroom is absolutely empty. The walls are bare; the floor is bare. There is neither furniture nor equipment.

The teacher enters, explains that for the next two weeks all equipment, books, and teachers will be taken from the classroom, and the teacher leaves. Attendance is required and you must decide what you will do. What would you study? Would it be worth studying? How would you go about it? How would you know if you learned anything? How useful would such learning be? What tools or skills would you need to study that you don't have now? Who knows about such tools or skills? Where did they learn them? What would scare you about such a learning time and subject? What would excite you? What would other people say?"

Children often have difficulty responding instantly, so you may lead some brainstorming on what they could learn. They usually begin listing activities concerned with external things, such as counting the number of squares on the floors, windows, and walls; progress to ideas involving ranking themselves according to height, hair color, eye color; eventually realize they could teach each other things that they know about; and finally begin to speak of their feelings, thoughts, and behaviors.

INTRODUCING FANTASY

The purpose of this activity is to help children to relax, to give free rein to the imagination, and to develop visual imagery.

NOTES FROM KAREN'S JOURNAL

I introduced myself and explained why I wanted to be a facilitator. We tried "Bumpety-Bump" with names. Everyone was excited and cooperative.

We also tried the activity using animal names and feeling words.

Student	Animal	Feeling
Karl	Horse	Tired
Norma	Rabbit	Mad
Arthur	Lion	Sad
Drew	Tiger	Tired
Mimi	Cheetah	I don't know—horrible
Joyce	Jaguar	Happy

continues on page 37

Notes from Karen's Journal, cont.

The games rose and fell in terms of attentiveness and noise. Patterns emerged: Karl always turned the game back so that he seldom had to be "It," until we finally encouraged him to stand up and take a turn. ("I have a way of always keeping my place.") He seems to have trouble listening. This may be part of the reason for his defensiveness. Mimi acted up throughout the class. She didn't really want to be "It", and her feeling word was "horrible." She disrupted the game by taking pillows and by kicking other people's pillows.

We introduced the idea of Self-Science, asking what each person thought might be learned from the group. Alice wrote this information on the board:

nothing; everything I can learn; experiences; about me

Notes from Karen's Journal

We began the class with a modified fantasy about what school would be like without furniture, teachers, or books. There was excitement and enthusiasm. A number of children had a very difficult time closing their eyes, but when asked what they could study they suggested:

"Walls" "Floor" "Hair" "Carpet"

"Eyes" "Lights" "Clothes"

"How to kill each other and ourselves"

No one mentioned feelings. We talked about whether learning about ourselves would be interesting and worthwhile, and whether it was something we did everyday. There were positive responses from some and negative responses from the older boys (typical of this age). We summarized by saying that Self-Science is a place where we could learn more about ourselves and others. We would do this through activities and experiments. Now there was considerable interest on the part of the older boys, who had been negative throughout the introduction.

I asked everyone what they'd do if they didn't have to go to school:

Jerry: Be sad.

George: I like school. I wouldn't have anyone to play with at home.

Arthur: Not a lot to do. This is a fun school. We have good activities.

Neal: It would be boring. No one to play with.

Peter: In a way, relieved, and in a way, sad. There wouldn't be anything to do. Just go downtown and look around. I wouldn't get an education.

Darby: During Christmas vacation, I really got bored. I was really happy to have the first day off, but then I got bored.

Sue: I'd feel bored.

Helga: If I had a choice, I'd go to school for three weeks and then have one week off.

Ally: Bored.

There was a definite pattern of "feeling bored if we couldn't go to school" and a pattern of liking school. The older boys "cut down" the program and expressed discontent. There was little in their response about feelings, thoughts, or other people. There is a need to legitimatize study of self and a need to explore and gain a better understanding of the dimensions of self and the possibilities for learning.

Lesson 3: Playing Games

BEGINNING

Review confidentiality (see pages 25 and 43, box).

Compare similarities in the group.

AFFECTIVE EXPERIENCE

- Just for fun, brainstorm games children already know and like. Choose any one, then play it. Play again with monitors.

- Discuss what we learned from this game. Ask questions pertinent to this game (see the discussion questions for Bumpety-Bump in Lesson 1). Ask "What did monitors see?"

COGNITIVE INQUIRY

1. "What are activities/games that are 'just for fun'? Do you like tag, hide and seek, hopscotch?"

2. "What do you learn about people who are strangers when you play a game?"

3. Focus on the value of games for learning. Ask "What can we learn from games? From football? From chess? From long distance running? Is this really learning?"

4. "What is a game in which you have to test your limits? What are the limits you test? Do you ever push your limits in your school work? In your relations with fellow students? Do you ever play games with yourself in which you test your limits, set goals, and try to reach them? What do you learn in this limit-testing? Is it important? Can someone else teach it to you?"

5. "Explain the difference between what you learn and how you learn it."

Lesson 4: Experiments

BEGINNING

Share the assignments students bring in. Introduce the concept of experimenting as a way of learning.

AFFECTIVE EXPERIENCE

- Distribute paper and pencils. Introduce this experiment: "If you were going to spend the rest of your life in this class, you would probably do some things differently and you might treat people differently. Write down two of these differences. Now, do one of these different things for the next ten minutes. How did your experiment with yourself turn out? What did you learn about yourself? Was that important learning? How did you do it?"

- Do additional experiments. Ask students to make a list of:

  a. three subjects you would find easy to talk about in this group;

  b. three subjects you would find hard to talk about;

  c. three subjects you would never want to talk about.

- Instruct students, "Do not write your name on your paper—make this list anonymous. Volunteer to turn in your anonymous list for discussion."

- Discuss similarities of lists; discuss awareness of subjects hard to talk about as a learning experience; discuss what makes these subjects hard to talk about.

- Introduce "Explode" (see Appendix C, page 153, and Karen's Journal, page 40). "Explode" at this point will probably be mild.

ASSIGNMENT

"Make a list of things you think you have learned in Self-Science so far — things you have learned about yourself or about someone else. How did you learn these things?"

MATERIALS

paper, pencils

COGNITIVE INQUIRY

1. "What did we just do? What have we learned about experimenting as a way of learning?"

2. "Did talking about the list of things you would never want to talk about change anybody's feelings about that?"

3. Discuss "exploding."

4. Ask, "are there any subjects that came up in the experiment today that the group would like to explore?"

5. Briefly explain the term consensus. See if you can get a consensus.

NOTES FROM KAREN'S JOURNAL

We reviewed "exploding" and discussed the limited ways and places we have to "explode."

Kelly told about the bomb that was placed at her front door to kill whomever opened the door. She said that it was done because her father is important. She said she is afraid of front doors. She went on for some time in great detail, but the group was very willing to listen.

Tim said he is afraid of TV antennas and footsteps on the roof. He explained that when he was six and living in the Chicago ghetto, there was a terrible riot on the night Martin Luther King was killed. There was a lot of shooting, with fires and sirens, etc., down the street. Tim was on the second floor, looking at TV with six adults and eight children. They heard someone on the roof and the person broke the TV antenna. At that time, a brick flew through the window, and Tim knew they had to try to get to the hospital a half-block away.

As they went out onto the street, a bomb exploded in the downstairs of their building, starting a fire. They went to the hospital amidst the gunfire and sirens and were in the emergency room with many wounded people when a man came in with a shotgun and started shooting. Tim fell on the floor and someone threw a tiny baby on him. He put the baby under him and crawled out a side door with the baby. Tim was able to talk very openly about how scared he was. He cried and had nightmares afterwards.

There was a lot of discussion by the rest of the group on how they would feel if that happened to them—what they would do, etc. They decided that one very common way of "exploding" for many people is violence; examples: war, riots, murders, beating-up people, hitting little kids. All of these ways hurt other people. We asked what different ways they could think of to explode without involving other people. They mentioned a room where they could hit pillows, throw bean bags, smash dishes (this was very intriguing), hit a punching bag, and play the game "Explode." They all decided to ask for a punching bag for Christmas.

We agreed to play "Explode." During the game, Kelly deliberately tripped Bruce, who fell and hurt himself. We stopped the game and everyone sat down. Bruce was trying not to cry.

Tim and Drew both told Kelly she should not have done that. She said that she didn't care because Bruce had knocked her down when they were playing football in P.E. There was much discussion about the difference between getting knocked down in a football game and during "Explode." Kelly was unwilling to give an inch. Bruce was very angry and hurt. He had a difficult time controlling his tears. I thought he was going to hit Kelly when it first happened.

Finally, I asked Bruce how he thought Kelly was feeling. He said, "Angry and hurt, because I knocked her down during football—even though it was an accident." I asked him what he thought would make her feel better. He replied, "If I said I'm sorry." When I asked him if he could do that, he said, "Yes. I'm sorry I knocked you down. I didn't do it deliberately."

I then asked Kelly how she thought Bruce felt. "Angry and hurt."

"Why?"

"Because I tripped him and he got hurt." I asked what could she do to make Bruce feel better, and she said, "Say I'm sorry. But I'm not." At this point she was put down by everyone in the group. I then asked her if she was sorry Bruce had really hurt his knee. "Yes."

"Could you tell him you're sorry about that?"

"I guess so. I'm sorry you got hurt, but I'm not sorry I did it." We were already ten minutes late so everyone had to leave at this point. We talked with Bruce for a few minutes and he was able to reduce some of his anger.

Approaching Goal 2

Developing a Trusting Attitude Toward Members of the Class

GROUP BEHAVIOR

These exercises in trust may generate the first examples of "testing" behavior from some of the students. You may see some defiance, refusal to participate, or attempts to change the subject. Should this occur, it is important to maintain a firm but accepting attitude and to understand the difficulty of learning to trust others. Remember that learning to trust often creates anxiety and that we all have our own ways of dealing with this anxiety. Expect some giggling and embarrassment during the Killer Statements exercises. Your acceptance will, of course, help the group feel more comfortable.

The level of trust, acceptance, and respect that a group develops usually determines the degree to which members of the group are willing to explore "self" as a subject. Take your cues from the group as you move from Goal 2 to 3.

Non-judgmental acceptance and respect is central to the process of personal growth. Indeed, it is central to simply hearing and seeing accurately, and thus learning. To put it another way, lack of trust generates defense mechanisms which get in the way of learning on any level.

Lessons 5 through 10 establish a basic trust among members of the group, as a foundation for the explorations to come. Cognitive awareness of how and why and when we trust or do not trust helps to focus on this subject. Lesson 6 should be given outdoors, if this can be arranged.

EVIDENCE OF AFFECTIVE GROWTH

- Increasing willingness to utilize all members of the class as partners in exercises.

- Increasing willingness to disclose personal feelings and concerns.

- Accepting and respecting the confidentiality of the class.

- Realizing the importance of trust, keeping confidences, accepting, and respecting.

EVIDENCE OF COGNITIVE GROWTH

- Using reading, writing, observing, classifying, and judgment skills in understanding trust.

- Learning ways of making decisions.

- Learning to classify by listening.

Lesson 5: Confidences

BEGINNING

Collect contracts. Discuss them. Use discussion questions to explore the subjects of trust and confidentiality. Discuss what aspects of Self-Science are appropriate to tell parents, other friends. Discuss what is not appropriate. Reassure students that this is a place where we can talk about things we cannot usually talk about elsewhere.

ASSIGNMENT

Give out student contracts to be decided upon and brought back next time. Here is a sample student contract.

Self-Science Contract

I _____(student's name)_____ , agree to participate in self-sciencing from now until the end of the year (or end of semester).

MATERIALS

journals, pens/pencils

AFFECTIVE EXPERIENCE

- Do the Nickname Experiment.
- Try the Telephone Gossip Chain Experiment.

COGNITIVE INQUIRY

1. Ask the discussion questions from the experiments (see "Questioning" page 22).

2. Introduce journals. Have students write answers to their questions before discussion.

3. Discuss how journals will be used (as scientists keep logs—to identify, observe, find patterns, etc.).

4. "What are some lessons from today? Where could you use them?"

Telephone Gossip Chain Experiment

PROCEDURE

Direct everyone to sit in a circle. Start a message around the circle by whispering to a student a sentence about yourself that the class doesn't know. The first student whispers the message to a second, and so on—with each person passing to the next whatever they hear. The last person in the chain tells the class what they heard, then the original sentence is shared. Ask questions while students are in the circle.

This exercise is used to examine patterns of listening.

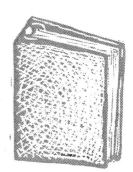

Additional Discussion Questions

1. "Was the final message the one that was started?"

2. "How did it change?"

3. "How well did you listen?"

4. "Is this a pattern of yours?"

PROCEDURE

Ask everyone to think of a nickname they have that they really do not like or that embarrasses them. Have everyone share their names and how they got them, and explain why they do not like them. (Teacher shares first.)

The Nickname Experiment

DISCUSSION QUESTIONS

1. "Is it easy/hard for you to trust people?"

2. "What did you like about the experiment?"

3. "What was scary about the experiment?"

4. "Who do you trust at school? At home? What makes you trust them?"

5. "What makes you feel as if you cannot trust some people? What do they do?"

Point out to the group that these names are confidential and, except for yours, may not be discussed outside the group. Also discuss the idea that there will be other feelings and thoughts we may want to share later on, such as things we are afraid of, and we will probably only do this if we feel sure others will keep this information confidential. (Note: We have never had a problem with this, but if a student should break this trust, it would be very important to deal with it as soon as possible, in the group. If there were a student who habitually broke the confidentiality of the group, it might be necessary to remove that person from the group and work with the person individually.)

NOTES FROM KAREN'S JOURNAL

We reviewed what we could learn in self-sciencing and whether it was important. We also discussed the conditions necessary to make the group work. Some of the reasons and conditions suggested by members of the group are:

REASONS

So we can learn to know ourselves.

So we can get to know people in the group well.

So we can gain self-confidence.

So we can learn to show feelings.

So we can come to understand our behavior.

CONDITIONS

We have to have trust.

We have to have confidentiality.

Gossiping about people is unacceptable.

At first the responses were vague, but eventually Bruce and Drew were able to explain the importance of learning about ourselves. The group was quiet and attentive, although Mimi moved about. I sat her down on my cushion.

In closing we asked the children to say how they felt right at the moment. Some felt tired (Karl). Norma was mad because Mimi was kicking and making noise. Mimi really heard her and acknowledged how Norma felt. Arthur also felt sad because everyone was noisy. The children were attentive to one another's feelings.

Impressions: It was an insightful and elating session. My personal anxiety is gone. The group is working. Mimi and Karl will be a real challenge. Their disruptive influence is strong; however, it is just as strongly balanced by the influence of the more serious, attentive ones (i.e., Norma, Bruce, Arthur and Drew).

Lesson 6: Trust

BEGINNING

Discuss the assignment. Talk about the level of trust in the group. Find out who feels excluded. Ask them to imagine what it would be like to be part of a group that had twice as much trust as this one does now.

ASSIGNMENT

Ask students to survey the friends and acquaintances they trust (least/most). (Show students a continuum of 1 to 5, 1 being the least, 5 being the most. Have them plot their findings on the continuum.)

AFFECTIVE EXPERIENCE

• Do the Trust Walk

COGNITIVE EXPERIENCE

1. "What **is** trust?"

2. "Why is trust important?"

3. "What does it take to increase trust? To decrease it?"

The Trust Walk Experience

PROCEDURE

Ask students to choose a partner, someone they would like to know better. Then blindfold one of each pair or ask the "blind" partners to close their eyes. Students lead their "blind" partners on a "Trust Walk." Give these instructions: "You have ten minutes to lead your partner around the yard (or classroom, school, gym, grounds, etc.) You are your partner's eyes, so establish a means of nonverbal communication (e.g., squeezing hands or lifting shoulders to indicate obstacles) to reinforce the words you use. Never leave your partner and make the walk as interesting as possible. At the end of ten minutes, switch roles and continue for the next ten minutes. Then return to the whole group."

FOLLOW-UP

Suggest that the partners discuss this experience, using the following processing questions as a "Trust Walk" guide. Reactions to the entire experience, noting high points, can be made in journals. Group discussion can follow.

This exercise provides an opportunity for students to enhance trust in themselves and others, and it increases sensory awareness.

DISCUSSION QUESTIONS

1. "How did you feel leading?"

2. "How did you feel following?"

3. "Which was easier?"

4. "Which was more fulfilling?"

5. "Were you scared?"

6. "When did you feel most secure?"

7. "How did it feel to have someone dependent on you? To depend on someone?"

8. "What did it feel like to be deprived of your sense of sight?"

BEGINNING

Talk about the assignment. Relate trust to acceptance and respect. What are some of the things that keep people from accepting and respecting each other? Elicit the group's ideas about put-downs.

Lesson 7: Watch Your Words

AFFECTIVE EXPERIENCE

- Do the Killer Statements Experiment.

COGNITIVE INQUIRY

1. "What are 'killer statements' or 'put-downs'?"

2. "How often do you hear them in this class? In school?"

3. "How does it make you feel when someone directs a killer statement at you?"

4. "How does it make you feel when you direct a killer statement at someone?"

5. "Why do you think people make killer statements?"

6. "Let's brainstorm and list all the killer statements we can think of."

7. "Make a list of all the words and phrases that you and others use to 'put down' others or to negatively judge them. Next to it make a list of all the words and phrases you use in praise or respect." For example:

Negative	Positive
dummy	tight
creep	cool

8. "How long is each list? Which group is more in use? Is there anything good about using the negative words and phrases? Which ones particularly get to you?"

9. "What would be the three worst things that anyone could say to you in here (say them to yourself in your head)?"

10. "What are the chances of getting through the day without anyone saying them? The year?"

11. "When people make killer statements in here, what is the effect on the class?"

12. "If no one in this class made any killer statements or put-downs for the rest of this week, what would happen? What would you personally get out of such a truce? What would you or the class lose?"

13. "What would happen if everyone stopped making killer statements? What would be good about it? What would be bad?"

ASSIGNMENT

Make a list of names in your journal of the people you feel you can trust.

Make a different list of all the killer statements you hear around school and at home. Include the killer statements you catch yourself saying.

The Killer Statements

(Put-Downs)

Experiment

This exercise is designed to help students become aware of hostile feelings—to learn that they are acceptable, normal emotions, and to discharge them without harming others.

PROCEDURE

Say to the students, "Everybody stand up. When I say, 'go,' all of you say or shout the killer statements you have held in until now. Use all the killer gestures, sounds, and words you want. You can talk to the air, to your neighbors, the whole group, your chair, or whatever feels comfortable."

DISCUSSION QUESTIONS

1. "What were your feelings as you were making the killer statements and gestures?"

2. "What or how did you feel after you made them?"

3. "Where in your body were those feelings?"

4. "Do you have any other comments about that exercise?"

5. "Did you like doing it?"

6. "How did you feel about waiting that long to make the killer statements and gestures? Was that feeling in your body somewhere?"

FOLLOW-UP

Journal entries

Small group sharing (e.g., dyads, triads, or "think/pair/share").

Group discussion

NOTES FROM KAREN'S JOURNAL

I explained Trust Walk to the group. Everyone picked a partner and had ten minutes for leading and ten minutes for following. I was impressed with how the leaders cared for their partners, introduced a great variety of touch experiences, as well as smell and taste (rocks, rough wall, glass, leaves, flowers, rope, grass, oranges, jasmine, dirt).

There was a definite mood of relaxation, easiness, and peace during the discussion. We talked about: How students felt leading/ following. They noticed a time change; the walk seemed longer when they were being led. Most of them thought it more fun to be led, easier to be the leader, and felt scared when not

in physical contact with their leader. No one expressed fear, although there was some uneasiness. I pointed out to Neal that he kept asking when it was time to stop and, at the end of the walk, took his mask off quickly. We talked at length about being deprived of sight as well as other senses.

We ended the group meeting by complimenting them on their skills as leaders and on their ability to trust themselves and each other. We suggested that we later talk more about trust and what it means. We also commented on how much we can communicate nonverbally through touch. It was a very positive day. I think we were all "high."

Lesson 8: Judgments

BEGINNING

Talk about the assignment. Introduce the term "judgments." Explain that judgments contain personal opinions and often involve comparisons. A judgment frequently becomes a decision and creates the impetus for action.

AFFECTIVE EXPERIENCE

- On chart paper, list all the ways we make judgments (from the homework). Brainstorm additional kinds of judgments.

- Categorize the list; what are some bases on which judgments are made (e.g., appearance, value, popularity).

COGNITIVE EXPERIENCE

1. "What are some good judgments you have made? Poor judgments?"

2. "How do you know if a judgment is good or not?"

3. "Who is most critical of you? You or someone else?"

4. "Do you give yourself permission to make mistakes, even if you 'look foolish'?"

5. "Reflecting on the judgments you have made, do you see a pattern? If so, what is the result of the pattern — what usually happens?"

6. "Could/should judgments be eliminated?"

7. "What are some lessons from today? Where else could you use them?"

ASSIGNMENT

During the week, keep a list of all the judgments you hear people making to each other (e.g., teachers judging students, students judging siblings, students judging each other). Also include judgments you make about others and about yourself.

MATERIAL

Chart paper, pens.

Lesson 9: Group Decisions

BEGINNING

Discuss what "consensus" means. Do decisions made by consensus meet everyone's needs? Discuss the concept of majority versus minority votes. Ask students to make a list of what is positive and what is negative about these two ways of making a decision.

AFFECTIVE EXPERIENCE

- Participate in the Consensus Experiment.

COGNITIVE INQUIRY

1. "How does consensus relate to acceptance and respect?"

2. "How do you know if you are accepted in here? Who decides? How do you know if you are rejected in here? Who decides?"

3. "Is the environment in the class basically accepting, positive, and respectful? Is your inner environment basically accepting, positive, and respectful of you?"

4. "Where do you feel most accepted and respected in your life? How does this make you feel? How do you perform there? How successful are you? How is this class different from that place?"

5. "What are the paths to acceptance in this class?"

6. "What are some of the ways people show acceptance and respect without words? Lack of acceptance and disrespect? Do you always know what you are communicating in this way? How can you learn what you are communicating without words?"

7. "What happens to people (children) who are not accepted by their parents? Teachers? How do you know? What can people do if they do not feel accepted or respected? What stops you from doing those things in here?"

NOTES FROM KAREN'S JOURNAL

We did the "Consensus Experiment" to decide if Shirley could join the group. Doug and Howard were negative, but the other children talked to them and they finally agreed. There were comments:

"How would you feel if you were Shirley?"

"Maybe you'd like her better if you got to know her."

"If she irritates you, you can talk about it here."

"I think they should have a better reason or Shirley can come."

"Your reasons sound personal."

"I think she should be in, if she wants to be."

We went out and brought Shirley in and Jay said, "Welcome to the group." We asked the class to tell her about our confidentiality agreement, the right to "pass" if you didn't want to say anything.

continues on page 49

The Consensus Experiment

PROCEDURE

Have the group sit in a circle. Explain that the group is going to paint this room/chair/table a different color, and that they need to get consensus on one color or combination of colors. Appoint a facilitator to go around the circle and ask each person to name a color; otherwise, only nonverbal communication is allowed.

After all colors are listed (once everyone has had a turn), the facilitator will, one color at a time, ask for a show of hands to indicate if the color is absolutely unacceptable to anyone. If any hands are raised, the facilitator will cross out that color.

It may be necessary to repeat the color-listing process.

During the experiment, students and teacher(s) should note the patterns of nonverbal communication and the styles of the participants. Who is aggressive, who goes along with the group or their best friend, who is frustrated, who are the leaders, who are the followers, and who pleads, orders, begs, or gets mad?

Use this technique often to make decisions within the group, e.g., should we have a visitor?

DISCUSSION QUESTIONS:

1. "How does it feel to make a decision by consensus? How would it have been different if we had voted?"

2. "Is consensus always practical? Why or why not?"

3. "How do these two methods of decision-making compare with having one person (e.g., teacher, parent, friend) making all the decisions?"

4. "Which do you prefer? Why?"

5. "What behaviors did you observe from the group?" (For example: some people were stubborn; some people changed easily; some people demanded; some people coaxed.)

6. "Is this how the group usually behaves? Does the group have a pattern it usually follows when making decisions?"

7. "What was your own behavior? Is this how you usually behave? Is this a pattern for you?"

NOTES FROM KAREN'S JOURNAL, CONT.

Shirley was reassured that she did not have to answer, but I wondered how she felt while she was waiting outside. I asked her, and her first response was, "Bored." Then she added, "I felt like I would not get in, because I do not have any friends in the group." Then she said she had some friends, but it was the boys who did not like her. I asked everyone to project themselves, to become Shirley and feel how she felt waiting to find out if she could be in our group. They had much to share:

"I would feel scared. I would feel like maybe no one would like me. I would feel uncomfortable. I would feel worried. I would feel like I waited and waited and waited."

Lesson 10: Acceptance

BEGINNING

This is a review of Goal 1 (Legitimizing Self-Knowledge as Valuable Subject Matter) and Goal 2 (Developing a Trusting Attitude Toward Members of the Class). Start by discussing trust, acceptance, and respect.

ASSIGNMENT

Tell three people what you respect them for today. Tell yourself three things you respect yourself for today.

When you feel like being sarcastic or putting someone down, don't! See if you can discover why you need to put that person down. Share what that need is, with the person or the class.

Note: You will not be processing this in depth. It is a gauge as to how open the group is now, prior to moving to the goal on feelings.

AFFECTIVE EXPERIENCE

- Try Bumpety-Bump variation with "Feelings."

COGNITIVE INQUIRY

1. "What are some of the ways people show acceptance and respect without words? Lack of acceptance and respect without words? Do you always know when you are communicating in this way? How can you learn what you are communicating without words?"

2. "Is there anything in your class other than the people that can cause someone to feel unaccepted or disrespected? What about the grading system? Competitive work schemes? Single standards for success, such as athletics for boys and appearance for girls?"

3. "Find a partner whom you most trust in the class and plan with his or her help to increase your own total acceptance and respect by doing something specific."

4. "Practice listening to the other students and just hearing and accepting them and their messages. Put off your ideas until another time; just focus on another person. Just hearing and accepting without 'yes, but,' 'that's dumb,' or stealing the focus with your concerns. This is the most acceptance-building thing one can do." (The teacher must be the model.)

5. "Brainstorm a list of things we can do to increase respect (e.g., when someone 'disses' you in some way, tell the person how you are feeling right then)."

6. "Brainstorm a list of things we can stop saying and doing that get in the way of creating respect (i.e., words, phrases, and actions to avoid because they hurt other people)."

7. "Review all the processes we have used so far to learn about ourselves (e.g., consensus, exploding, experimenting, fantasy, asking questions, talking, nonverbal cues, etc.)."

Approaching Goal 3

Becoming More Aware of Multiple Feelings

GROUP BEHAVIOR

The group should begin to bond together more now. Exercises in the next lessons enhance the awareness of feelings. This period of time can be a very pleasant, growing time for the group.

EVIDENCE OF AFFECTIVE GROWTH

- Increasing ability to inventory one's thoughts and feelings.

- Increasing awareness of the relationship between one's emotions and physical states.

- Increasing willingness to listen to others.

- Increasing acceptance and support of the thoughts and feelings of others in the class.

- Increasing awareness of the similarities and differences between one's own unique response to an experience and the responses of others.

Experiencing one's self and one's surroundings is central to learning. Awareness of feelings, one's own and others', deepens learning about personal relationships, communication, language arts (tone, mood, character, inference, and predictions in reading).

Children are often aware of their strong feelings, but have difficulty discriminating among more subtle emotional states. They need a vocabulary for feelings and an understanding of the various modes of expression to make choices about this important aspect of their learning and growth. People neither think without feeling nor feel without thinking. Connections on this point need to be made.

Remember to schedule OASIS lessons through these next weeks (see Appendix E, page 158).

EVIDENCE OF COGNITIVE GROWTH

- Developing vocabulary for expressing and describing feelings.

- Understanding concepts of the process of feelings; labeling feelings.

- Understanding the relevance of feelings to self, home, and school (i.e., understanding feelings of friends, siblings, characters from books, etc.).

- Understanding various modes of perceiving feelings.

- Acknowledging the responsibility for one's own feelings.

START WITH YOU

*Continue to encourage awareness of feelings and ways of identifying feelings. Model this skill by tuning into **yourself** through introspection and/or fantasy; by nonverbal cues; by behaviors/actions. Share your observations with your students.*

Lesson 11: Naming Feelings

BEGINNING

When the students come in, ask them, "How do you feel? How are you feeling today?" If they respond without detail (e.g., "fine"), discuss why that happens. Ask them why people greet one another with "how are you feeling?" and answer "fine" even when they are not fine?

MATERIALS

3 x 5 index cards (approximately 100)

PREPARATION

Before the class begins, draw a "feeling continuum" on the chalkboard.

Example:

Angry   Upset   Sad/Calm   Indifferent   Bored   Happy   Excited

FOLLOW-UP

Brainstorm feelings — all the words the class can think of. Ask for volunteers to write the words on the board. Ask for other volunteers to write feeling words on 3 x 5 cards, one word to a card. Explain that for the next few lessons we will be collecting feeling words and making experiment cards.

Help the brainstorming by suggesting categories of feelings (i.e., good feelings, bad feelings, loving feelings, and neutral feelings). Teachers should add some complex words (e.g., embarrassed, content, indifferent).

Do not expect a long list at first. The list will grow with awareness and time.

active	curious	glum	itchy	proud	stupid
angry	dejected	good	joy	put-down	surprised
bad	depressed	great	joyful	puzzled	terrible
boiling	down-in-	hateful	kind	rage	thankful
bold	the-dumps	happy	lazy	rich	thin
brave	embar-	helpful	like-an-	sad	tired
bruised	rassed	helpless	idiot	safe	unhappy
careful	energy	hot	love	scared	unimpor-
chicken	enjoy	hurt	mad	shocked	tant
clumsy	excited	hysterical	mean	shy	unpro-
cold	fat	important	miserable	sick	tected
comfort-	fine	impressed	nauseated	silly	upset
able	flattered	in-between	needed	sleepy	warm
content	free	happy and	nice	sly	weak
cowardly	frightened	sad	nuts	smart	wealthy
crazy	furry	indifferent	overjoyed	sorry	weird
cuckoo	glad	invisible	poor	strong	well

AFFECTIVE EXPERIENCE

- Ask students to indicate how they feel right now (present feeling state) by putting initials under those feeling words on the chalkboard. Have them add any word that better describes their feelings.

- Use present feeling states to introduce The Martian Fantasy.

- Ask discussion questions that focus on feelings.

COGNITIVE INQUIRY

1. "What did we just do?" (Become aware of feelings.)

2. "Are feelings easy or hard to talk about? What makes it hard to talk about them?"

3. "How do you know when you're feeling a feeling? Can you stop or change your feelings? Increase your feelings?"

4. "What are some lessons from today? Where else could you use them?"

The Martian Fantasy

PROCEDURE

Begin with a fantasy induction method like deep breathing or a relaxation technique (e.g., "Imagine that you are sitting by the beach listening to the waves...") Introduce the Martian Fantasy: "Imagine that you are here at school and you see a flying saucer. It comes closer and closer and finally lands in the parking lot. There are blinking lights and strange sounds. A door opens and a strange creature emerges. It approaches the school and finds a place to enter. It has come to observe how we talk to each other. (Long pause.)

"What kinds of words would it hear? What kinds of positive things would it hear us saying to each other? For example, I like you; that is a nice drawing; I appreciate you for helping me with my math; you are a good friend. What kinds of killer statements (i.e., negative statements or put-downs) would it hear us saying? For example, You are stupid; I don't like you; You're not my friend; I'm going to hit you. How do we say what we say? What kinds of words do we use?"

This activity can be used with any aspect of communication. It's a good way to introduce "praise" or to stimulate a continued discussion on killer statements.

NOTES FROM KAREN'S JOURNAL

We asked the children to list all the words they knew for feelings after telling them "The Martian Fantasy." How many words would the Martian hear?

Happy	Merry	Disliked
Sad	Unhappy	Cool
Confused	Scared	Hot
Mad	Sticky	Great
Angry	Soft	Dull
Joy	Hard	Sleepy

Then we asked them how they could tell the Martian (who didn't know our language) what these words meant. They acted out some of the words while the rest of the group tried to guess the meanings.

Lesson 12: What Are Feelings?

BEGINNING

Share the new feeling words students have collected for homework. Explain that there are eight basic feelings (fear, anger, joy, sadness, acceptance, disgust, expectation, and surprise) with hundreds of shades, variations, and combinations in between.

ASSIGNMENT

Start listening for feeling words at school and at home. Come in with at least one **new** feeling word next time.

MATERIALS

3x5 index cards; straight pins

AFFECTIVE EXPERIENCE:

- Use the cards to introduce the Milling Around Experiment. Each child should try to act out the word on his/her card. A student may put back any s/he finds too difficult.

COGNITIVE INQUIRY

Process what feelings were easy to act out. Which were hard? What is a feeling anyway? (Give a brief explanation of the limbic brain and that feelings are electro-chemical signals in the nerves.)

1. "What could we learn from knowing about feelings?" (Understanding other people better, descriptions in books and poetry, society, etc.)

2. "Can expressing feelings get you in trouble? When have you gotten in trouble expressing feelings? Are you having any feelings right now that would be risky to express? What are the feelings which people have gotten in trouble for expressing?" (e.g., anger, frustration, love, affection, hate, hope.)

NOTES FROM KAREN'S JOURNAL

We introduced the Milling Around Experiment and the children were very involved for about ten minutes portraying an angry child, a critical parent, an unhappy little child, a pouting child, a crying child, a joyful child. We had an opportunity to introduce new vocabulary and observe how freely each child was able to express feelings in nonverbal ways. We spent time discussing which feelings were the easiest, and which the hardest, to express.

3. "When you don't express a feeling, what happens to it? Does it just go away? What do you lose by not expressing a feeling? Do you remember a time when you didn't express a feeling and lost something by it?"

4. "What feelings are in this room right now? What difference does it make? What good does it do for a teacher to know how a student is feeling? A parent? A friend?"

Continue discussion of ways we can learn more about feelings.

PROCEDURE

Collect feeling words by having a volunteer write them on the board. Ask another volunteer to write each on a card. Shuffle the cards and deal out one to each person.

Have students pin or tape the card to themselves and stand in the class space in the center of the room. Direct students to start milling (walking slowly) around the room, showing their feeling on faces. After approximately two minutes, stop the milling and ask them to analyze their styles of participation:

> "Stop and think for a second about the way you walked."
>
> "Did you walk towards the center of the group, or stay on the periphery?"
>
> "Did you walk fast or slow?"
>
> "Did you feel as if you were following someone?"
>
> "Did you feel as if you were being followed?"
>
> "Did you change direction/pace at all?"
>
> "Did you look at people while you were walking?"
>
> "Did you make contact with others in any way?"
>
> "How did you feel about the people you 'met' when you were milling?"
>
> "Did you feel the feeling word on your card? On anybody else's card?"

After giving people a few moments for processing their own responses, ask them to start milling again. Stop the milling after approximately one or two minutes, and ask the following "thought" questions:

> "Were there any changes in the way you walked during the second half of the exercise?
>
> Did you change the way in which you made contact or did not make contact with the people you 'met' while milling?
>
> Was there anything that you wanted to do that you did not permit yourself to do in this exercise?"

FOLLOW-UP

Make and discuss journal entries. Lead group discussion of reactions to exercise.

The Milling Around Experiment

This is an exercise in low-level risk taking which will generate data about patterns of interaction with others.

VARIATIONS

Have students wear blindfolds and mill. Then have them mill with eyes open. Focus on differences between the two experiences, the ways in which contact was made (or not made) blindfolded or with eyes open.

Lesson 13: Reading Body Language

BEGINNING

Discuss nonverbal communication and how we know what people are feeling.

AFFECTIVE EXPERIENCE

- Play "charades" acting out emotion words.

COGNITIVE INQUIRY

Ask questions to elicit awareness of body talk as one way of learning about feelings. Encourage children to discuss sending and receiving as part of communication. Discuss what is sent (the message) and how it is sent (words, body language, tone) and the connotation or "subtext" (the feelings underlying the message, the unintentional message).

1. "What are some kinds of nonverbal communication?" (Body language, tone, expression, sounds, gestures.)

2. "How much of our communication is nonverbal?" (About 85% of emotional content is communicated nonverbally.)

3. "Can we say one thing and express an opposing feeling nonverbally? Where? When? How?"

4. "What are some lessons from today? Where else could you use them?"

Help students focus on what others are communicating to them and what they are communicating to others. This will allow them to be more effective in their communications and expand their repertoire of communication skills.

Lesson 14: Emotional Symbolism

BEGINNING

Ask everyone to share the magazine pictures they have brought in. Emotions can be wrapped-up in pictures and symbols — like they are in nonverbal communication (Lesson 13).

AFFECTIVE EXPERIENCE

- Spend the lesson starting a "feelings" collage which will stay in the classroom.

Provide many magazines, interesting pictures, scissors, and glue with which the students can work. Have them go through magazines and create a collage of themselves on the poster boards (or construction paper). The pictures that the children choose may be a representation of their feelings. For example, a picture of a beat-up car represents the feeling of being hurt or picked on.

Working in small groups is preferable, but let children work individually if they wish. Each child then explains to the class what his/her representation is about; members of the class and the teacher are allowed to ask clarifying questions.

COGNITIVE INQUIRY

1. "What do your pictures say about you?"

2. "Do your friends know this side of you?"

3. "If you were to have done this activity a year ago, how would it have been different? What if you do it a year from now?"

ASSIGNMENT

Collect magazine or newspaper pictures that show some kind of feeling. Objects can generate feelings, such as a lonely city, a scary night. Choose any pictures that have some feeling for you. Label the feeling.

MATERIALS

Magazines, pictures, scissors, glue, poster-board or construction paper for each child.

Lesson 15: Evoking Emotions

BEGINNING

Review ideas of how emotions can be attached to pictures and nonverbal communication. Ask why it is useful to know lots of words for feelings.

ASSIGNMENT

Bring in your favorite tape or CD, preferably a song with lyrics.

AFFECTIVE EXPERIENCE

- Have students take turns playing the music that they have brought. Ask each student to tell why he or she chose that song, what feeling it evokes in them. Elicit similarities and differences in feelings.

- Play some of the music and encourage children to move to the music as they listen.

MATERIALS

stereo/"boom box", 3 x 5 index cards

COGNITIVE INQUIRY

1. "Did you learn more words for feelings? (List and put on cards as before.) How do you usually learn more words for feelings? Is this useful learning? How?"

2. "Do you often discover how you are feeling by other people's expressions of their feelings?"

3. "Have you learned anything about your feelings today? This week? Is this real learning? Where else do you learn such things? (Offer books, films, television, and social interactions as other sources of learning about feelings.) What if feelings were outlawed? Would we be better off without them? In what ways?"

NOTES FROM KAREN'S JOURNAL

The group agreed to meet during their lunch period Thursday because a field trip was planned. They had missed the previous two weeks because of half-day sessions and they were very upset.

Everyone ate lunch while we talked. We discussed our session with Lou Savery the week before and it was interesting to see how much the children remembered. We talked at length about altered states of consciousness and the fact that there are many inner spaces to explore and many "elevators" (Lou's term) to get us there. The students remembered: drugs, yoga, meditation, hypnosis, and music. We reviewed Peter's unpleasant memory state, which he shared today. Today, Peter happened to hear the same music being played that a friend and he had played one night at his friend's house, when he felt really weird things were happening. When he could not change his state and no longer wanted to be there, he opened his eyes. We again pointed out that with music as an "elevator," he had choices, but if he had taken a drug, for example, he would have had to wait until the drug wore off.

continues on page 59

Close by pointing out that we have been naming words for feelings, seeing feelings in pictures, hearing feelings in music. Continue this discussion with, "Is listening important? Why?"

You may wish to close this lesson by repeating an active experiment like Explode or Milling Around.

Lesson 16: Acting on Emotions

BEGINNING

Ask students to add new feeling words to cards. Introduce the idea of "inventory." Spend a few minutes inventorying the cards collected so far into categories of: Pleasure/Love; Pain/Hate words.

When the cards have been sorted, ask students what feelings they have at this very moment. Also express your feelings.

AFFECTIVE EXPERIENCE

- Complete the Video Camera Experiment, sending messages about present feelings. Questions focus on receiving messages (i.e., listening).

- Try variations of acting out feeling cards, or Bumpety-Bump with feelings, or a charades relay race.

COGNITIVE INQUIRY

Having developed awareness of feelings and ways they can be expressed, the focus now moves to accepting responsibility for one's own feelings.

1. "Did you ever have a feeling that you did not understand or resolve? Do you have such feelings often? Do others have them too? How do you know if others are having the same difficulties with feelings that you are?"

2. "Do feelings ever make people sick? How? Do people really get headaches and ulcers from feelings?"

3. "Some say that each person has a 'duffel bag' into which all the sad, angry, frustrated feelings are put. We all have them every day but we don't express them. Then when someone (usually close friends or family who won't fight back) does something the least bit annoying, we dump the 'duffel bag' all over her or him. Have you ever dumped your saved-up bad feelings on an undeserving friend? Has this ever happened to you? What did you

continues on page 60

ASSIGNMENT

Ask the group to keep listening to people's feelings at school and home and to bring in another new word for the list.

MATERIALS

3 x 5 index cards

NOTES FROM KAREN'S JOURNAL, CONT.

Jim began to tell about his dreams, particularly the ones that seemed to come true a week or two later. There were many agreements and lots of dream-sharing about scary things—dying, funny dreams, dreams of being attacked and jumped on, dreams of wishing to be somewhere else. We also discussed length of dreams and I told about a class I took where I studied dreams. Everyone thought it would be fun to keep a dream journal in order to remember dreams for sharing and discussing. I suggested that dreams were coded messages and if we could decipher the code we might understand ourselves better. Dana observed that while we were all sharing dreams, she realized how similar people really are. Not just that they have similar dreams, but that they are similar in many other ways, too.

Today was a great day. There was a close group feeling. Everyone but Sue was actively interested and we really were anxious to meet again. It was good feedback to hear them all complain about missing self-sciencing, really liking it, and being willing to meet during lunch so they wouldn't have to miss a session.

LESSON 16, COGNITIVE
INQUIRY, CONT.

do? How did you feel?"

4. "Do you have any 'unfinished' situations you are carrying around with you today? A quarrel with your parent this morning that you are still angry or sad about? An incident with a classmate that didn't turn out fairly or left you frustrated? Have you been planning for any situation that you have strong feelings about? What is the effect of these leftover feelings on what you've been doing today? If the effect isn't good, how can you free yourself from these leftover feelings? How long can a leftover feeling influence you? Do you sometimes still feel sad over a lost friend from a year ago? Can you recall a success or a happy feeling from it?"

The Video Camera Experiment

This is a good activity to help children develop listening skills.

PROCEDURE

One child gives a short message (the subject can be open-ended or directed; e.g., "something I feel proud about," "what I like most/least," "something important to me"). Then this same child picks a member of the group to be the video camera. S/he must repeat back word-for-word the message. You can increase the difficulty by making the message longer, adding facial expressions, tone of voice, body movements, rate of speech, etc.

NOTES FROM KAREN'S JOURNAL

We found our space again in the Ballet Room. I think the mirrors in there are magic, making all of us more aware of our expressions, our movements, and of each other.

I asked Bob to be the scribe for the group, which he did with seriousness and pleasure. We all thought of words to describe our feelings after an initial romp around the room to relieve body tensions. We stamped, skipped, and hopped, the only verbalization being laughter. We talked a bit about expressing feelings through movement. The words for feelings came freely: uptight, happy, excited, angry, tired, confused, shy, sad, relaxed, weird.

We acted out nonverbally: How do you feel today? (Video Camera) Bob volunteered first; stomped around, snorted, threw himself on the floor and pounded with his fists, all in high good humor. Dana is thoughtful, moving around and tipping her ponytailed head like a miniature princess. Alice skips, she feels happy. Several show how tired they are. One is bored. We extend the actions into words and discuss how the movements convey feelings. "How would you label such a feeling?" Interpretations vary. Lila acted shy, which no one understood (some saw it as fear); so, we all tried being shy in her manner. Beth tried to be shy or tired but could not, which led to the closing discussion about how difficult it really is to understand someone else's feelings.

Lesson 17: Sources of Feelings

BEGINNING

Introduce concepts: perceptions, judgments, and values.

Draw a feeling continuum on the chalkboard as in Lesson 11. This time don't put on labels. Ask students to label and indicate their feelings at the present moment.

Discuss any past or present causes for the individual feelings (e.g., "happy because I'm going on a trip this weekend"; "sad because my goldfish died"; "hassled because I had a fight with my father this morning").

AFFECTIVE EXPERIENCE

- From any of the feeling situations raised, ask the group to choose some they would like to role-play.

- Teach the group how to role play and act out several of the situations. (See Role-Playing, page 23.)

ASSIGNMENT

Make a drawing of any thing that you think most expresses your feeling about yourself and your present mood (i.e., draw an animal, tree, flower, food, etc.)

COGNITIVE INQUIRY

Discuss the role-plays.

1. "Does this happen often? How does it start?"

Trace the situation through the feeling response. Introduce the idea of a pattern, a characteristic way of responding.

2. "Who/what causes your feelings? Many wise people have suggested that when we recognize and assume responsibility for our own feelings we are in control and do not blame others."

3. "Is it important for us to hear about someone's feeling even though that is not our feeling? What would make this important? Are we taking responsibility for our feelings when we identify them for the class? How? Is this useful to us?"

Explain to the class that sometimes expressing feelings can be an attempt to cause someone to do or say something that the expresser wants.

If you think someone is expressing feelings to influence you in a certain way, ask them directly if it is true. For example, "Are you saying you are feeling lonely so I'll invite you to come to the party we're planning?"

Expressing feelings is often helpful, but you shouldn't expect people to guess what you want from your expression. Experiment with saying what you need directly to the person who can meet that need, in addition to naming your feelings.

Lesson 18: Responsibility for Feelings

BEGINNING

Share and discuss feeling situations the students encounter. Continue to discuss the idea of patterns (characteristic ways of responding) begun in Lesson 17.

ASSIGNMENT

Watch for any situation that gives you a strong feeling. Write down a description of the situation and what feeling you had.

AFFECTIVE EXPERIENCE

- Try a variation of "Bumpety-Bump" with feelings; choose and act out the feelings which surfaced in the homework assignment. Switch to present feelings. Note whether feelings changed.

COGNITIVE INQUIRY

1. "Try this exercise: Name your present feeling and then say to yourself, 'I'm making myself feel _____ (angry, sad, alone) right now.' See how often you can believe this sentence.

    When it really seems as if someone is causing a feeling in you, say to yourself, 'I'm allowing _____ (Bill, Sue, etc.) to act as a catalyst and I am making myself feel _____ (happy, mad, lonely, etc.).'"

2. "What did you learn from this experiment? What was the most difficult part about it for you? What did you say to yourself to avoid the experiment?"

During this lesson, introduce the Trumpet Process as a way of looking at ourselves. Show how we can use the Trumpet Process to see what we've been learning about feelings. Go through the first three steps— share experiences; inventory responses; recognize patterns (see page 12).

Approaching Goal 4

Developing Communication Skills for Affective States

GROUP BEHAVIOR

(See Appendix C, page 151.) During the lessons, you may want to adjust focus depending on the progress of the group. If the group has opened up and expressed the feeling states described in Goal 3, progress in sequence through the lessons, emphasizing cognitive inquiry and the verbalization of communication skills. If the group development process seemed slow, or if the group had difficulties on the earlier lessons, focus more on the affective parts of the lessons. Allow for more experiences in recognizing and expressing feelings.

In Goal 3, students concentrated on simply becoming aware of and labeling feeling states. Now they move into two new areas: an awareness of their present feeling state (i.e., recognizing their own feelings clearly at any given moment), and learning how to communicate about feelings (expressing their own feelings as well as receiving communication of others' feelings). This involves observing the discrepancies between a sender's words, tone of voice, and body language. Also, cognitive inquiry continues, using experiences on which to build abstractions by cataloging the subject matter in terms of the Trumpet Process, Steps 1, 2, and 3. Lessons 19 through 23 concentrate on communication skills.

EVIDENCE OF AFFECTIVE GROWTH

- Accepting new procedures for learning (e.g., fantasizing, role-playing, nonverbal communication, etc).

- Improving listening skills and self-expression.

- Developing additional vocabulary.

- Relaxing and creating visual imagery.

EVIDENCE OF COGNITIVE GROWTH

- Developing interpretation and inference skills.

- Distinguishing between fact and judgment.

- Learning the concept of negotiation in problem situations.

- Understanding that communication includes both sending and receiving.

ZONES OF AWARENESS

Everyone cycles on a continuum of awareness within relatively distinct zones— inner, middle, outer. The inner zone consists of physical situations and feelings of the body itself.

The middle zone consists of memories, fantasies, planning, thinking, etc. or what is commonly called mental activity.

The outer zone consists of the sensations which come from outside one's skin.

Have the students try to pay attention to the continuum of awareness. Some people are able to pay attention to two zones at the same time. Usually it's easy to name the focus of one's attention; the challenge is to observe yourself to see habitual patterns in terms of the continuum of awareness.

Lesson 19: Being Emotionally Present

BEGINNING

Ask students to sit in a circle. Introduce the idea of being "emotionally present" or paying attention to the "here-and-now." Talk about knowing when one is in touch with the "here-and-now."

ASSIGNMENT

Look for strong feeling situations and name them to yourself. Identify two such incidents and write them in your journal.

AFFECTIVE EXPERIENCE

- Complete the Hot Potato Feeling Experiment.

COGNITIVE INQUIRY

Ask the discussion questions included with the "Hot Potato." Categorize the feelings (i.e., inner zone, middle zone, outer zone).

1. "Was there a preponderance of one zone over another?"

2. "Is this a common pattern for you?"

3. "What zone of feelings might you share with your friends? Family? Strangers?"

The Hot Potato Feeling Experiment

PROCEDURE

Have students pair off and play "Hot Potato" with an object they can toss back and forth (e.g., bean-bag, hacky-sack, tennis ball). When students get the "Hot Potato" they have to say what they are feeling right now, then toss the potato to their partner. This action continues for several minutes—even if students find it hard.

FOLLOW-UP

Aloud, or in journals, respond to the discussion questions.

DISCUSSION QUESTIONS

1. "Is this experiment hard or easy? What do you think makes it hard or easy?"

2. "How does it feel to have to say what you are feeling? How do you feel when you can't say anything?"

3. "Is there anything you would like to have said but censored instead? What?"

VARIATION

Follow the same proceedure but in a larger group. This stimulates paying attention and gives a greater range of feelings.

This exercise gives learners practice in inventorying their feelings.

Lesson 20: Zones of Emotions

BEGINNING

Sitting in a circle, discuss strong feelings categorized on the homework assignment. Review "here-and-now" concepts.

Review vocabulary: metaphors, zones, habitual patterns, learning, brainstorming, etc.

AFFECTIVE EXPERIENCE

- Participate in the Feeling Chain Experiment and Role-Playing-Feeling Metaphors Experiment.

COGNITIVE INQUIRY

1. "What are habitual patterns? How do habitual patterns serve you? In what zone of awareness do you spend the most time? What zone is best for studying? Playing Monopoly? Baseball? Sleeping? Communicating with friends?"

2. "What can't you do if you're not aware of the outer zone? What is it like to be deaf? Blind? Without a sense of touch? Are you sometimes 'out of touch' with the outer zone? How do you really know when someone sees or hears you?"

ASSIGNMENT

In your journal, categorize three strong feelings you experience. See if you can identify which zone the feelings come from.

MATERIALS

newsprint and magic markers, or a board

The Feeling Chain Experiment

PROCEDURE

Divide the class into groups of four to six. Each person takes a card and writes a core feeling on it. Pass the cards to the right, and have each person write a related word. Pass the cards quickly around, over and over.

This activity is valuable for increasing affective vocabulary and improving inventorying skills— particularly feelings and sensations.

DISCUSSION QUESTIONS

1. "What kinds of words were easy for you to link with?"

2. "Were you concerned with how others would respond to your words?"

3. "Did you censor yourself?"

4. "Do we all mean the same thing by the same words?"

VARIATIONS

Related words can be "shades" of the original word; "joy" −> "happy" −>"content" −> "exuberant"

Related words can be metaphors: "joy" −> "sunshine" −>"swingset" −> "daisies"

The activity can be done aloud, on cards, or on chart paper.

Role-Playing-Feeling-Metaphors Experiment

This exercise will help students both with self-disclosure and in their search for patterns.

PROCEDURE

Have the children act out some of the feeling metaphors they brainstormed without using any words. They should choose a metaphor from the lists, and write the title on the board (e.g., "eggbeater"). As they role-play the feeling, the audience observes the feelings of the actor and of themselves and tries to identify specifics of where and how the feeling is expressed.

DISCUSSION QUESTIONS

For the role-player, ask: "How did your body feel as an *(eggbeater)*? Where in your body did you feel this? Did you notice your body (e.g., clenched fists, crouched position, etc.)? What did you do with different parts of your body? How did they feel?"

For the audience, ask: "What did *(student's name)* do that made you feel s/he was feeling *(frustrated)*? How do you think s/he felt? How accurate were your observations of the feelings?"

FOLLOW-UP

Have the children in the audience describe what they saw, and how they imagine the role-playing student felt. Have a discussion either after each role-play or after all the role-plays, using the Trumpet Process questions to guide the discussion.

Children who are reluctant to role-play their feeling metaphor can describe/tell their partner, support group, or class about the metaphor.

After all the role-plays, ask questions for students to respond to in their journals, and then share their answers.

VARIATIONS

This exercise may be role-played with a partner in support groups. After each role-play, ask the person questions to help analyze the feelings.

After all students complete their role-plays, ask questions for the students to respond to in their journals. Then the students can share, either again with partners, or support groups, or the whole class.

Students can also role-play feeling metaphors without first writing them on the board. Other students can try to identify the feelings from the nonverbal cues.

Lesson 21: Multiple Emotions

BEGINNING

Discuss how we experience some emotions in different parts of our bodies (e.g., butterflies in the stomach for nervousness, tight shoulders for stress).

Review vocabulary words, and add new ones: perceptions, concepts, awareness, preference, satisfaction, senses, etc.

AFFECTIVE EXPERIENCE

- Here-and-Now Statements.
- Here-and-Now Wheel Experiment.

COGNITIVE INQUIRY

1. "How aware are you of your middle zone of thoughts, memories, and fantasies?"
2. "Are there some thoughts that you have over and over?"
3. "Do you spend a lot of time planning? When?"
4. "How often are you aware of your feelings? Your inner zone?"
5. "Strong feelings usually force themselves to our attention, but do you ever deliberately check out your body, your inner zone, to see what is happening with your feelings? Check now!"

ASSIGNMENT

In your journal, identify three feelings, and indicate where in your body you felt them.

MATERIALS

newsprint and magic markers for each student.

NOTES FROM KAREN'S JOURNAL

We were able to return to the "here-and-now" to talk. Heidi suggested we tell about our sicknesses and scary things. Taylor agreed, but he also wanted to talk about death. He is afraid of dying. Everyone agreed that it was a concern. Eric is going to be a doctor when he grows up and he will discover a pill that will help us live forever.

We asked if there were any other topics people would like to talk about. Eric wanted to talk about "asking stupid questions." We were able to help him clarify that he sometimes feels stupid when he asks questions. The other children told him he should not feel that way; that he had to ask questions to learn. We all agreed to think of a question we would feel stupid asking, and that we would talk about it next time.

Here-And-Now Statements Experiment

PROCEDURE

Have students sit in a circle. Explain the rule that for this exercise only things happening at the moment can be mentioned. Go around the circle having each student complete the statement, "Right now I see...." Each has the option of passing. Repeat, using "Right now I hear", "Right now I am touching", "Right now I feel", "Right now I am aware..."

This activity will increase awareness of perceptions and feelings as they are being experienced.

DISCUSSION QUESTIONS

1. "Did you become aware of anything you normally wouldn't have noticed?"

2. "What usually gets in the way?"

3. "What helped your awareness here?"

4. "How many different senses can you attend to at one time?"

5. "Are certain combinations of senses easier for you than others?"

6. "Do you attend to certain senses more than others?"

7. "Does this match up with some of your patterns?"

8. "Are there alternatives that might be useful for you?"

FOLLOW-UP

Group sharing of "I learned . . ." statements can be useful in illustrating some of the here-and-now experiences that usually go consciously unnoticed. Brainstorm with the group some of the factors that affected their awareness positively or negatively. Discuss the advantages and disadvantages of heightening consciousness to so many stimuli.

Procedure

Have the students each draw a circle with four spokes so that the circle is divided into four quarters. Label each quarter with a different "area" of feelings, for instance, "family," "friends," "public," "private." (See Figure 6.)

Next have them write a word for each quarter which describes how they are feeling right now. Then take one of those words and expand it into two sentences.

Here-and-Now Wheel Experiment

Discussion Questions

1. "Are your present feelings typical of your day-to-day feelings?"

2. "Did you get in touch with any feelings that surprised you?"

3. "Are you satisfied with the way you are feeling? If not, what could you do to change your feelings in the direction you'd prefer? Do others feel as you do?"

This activity increases awareness of the variety of feelings students may be experiencing at any given moment, broadening the perception of those feelings.

Follow-up

Using paper and magic markers, have the children depict their feelings, emphasizing the one feeling they expanded.

Ask students to make another wheel that would have just the opposite feelings; then compare the two wheels in respect to your preferences, pleasantness, satisfaction, goals, etc.

With the class divided into triads, have them share what they wish from the here-and-now wheels.

Group members can volunteer to share with the whole class what they wish from their wheels.

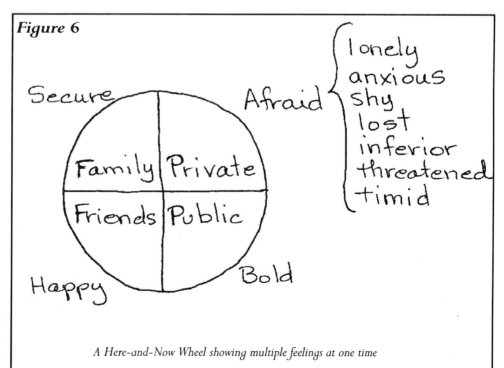

Figure 6

Secure   Afraid   lonely anxious shy lost inferior threatened timid

Family | Private

Friends | Public

Happy   Bold

A Here-and-Now Wheel showing multiple feelings at one time

Lesson 22: Sharpening Observation

ASSIGNMENT

Observe your morning "ritual." In your journal, carefully list everything you do in the half-hour after you wake up. Note which items are ones you almost always do.

BEGINNING

Discuss the last session. Was anything learned? Five minutes into the class, ask these questions:

"What have you been doing in the last five minutes?"

"What have you been feeling?"

"Have your feelings changed in that time?"

"What have you been thinking?"

"What were you saying to yourself in your head?"

"What did you learn about yourself just now?"

Discuss meaning of new vocabulary (e.g., attending, perception, nonverbal cues).

Do the Telephone Gossip Chain Experiment (page 42).

AFFECTIVE EXPERIENCE

- The Nonverbal Gossip Experiment.
- The I Witness Experiment.

COGNITIVE INQUIRY

1. "Identify skills that were useful for these experiments."
2. "Write in your journal five communication skills. What do the terms mean?"
3. "Can you learn about yourself by studying yourself? How?"
4. "What tools do scientists use to study cells? Do people need tools to study themselves?"
5. "What if you were to do exactly the opposite of what you're doing right now? What would you be doing?"

Procedure

Students sit in a circle. One student volunteers to express a feeling nonverbally to the one next to him/her, who passes it on to the next, and so on until it goes all around the circle. Invite one student to choose a rumor that exists in the group and express it nonverbally. Try several rounds and variations of the exercise.

The Nonverbal Gossip Experiment

This exercise offers experience in attending, perception, and nonverbal communication skills.

Discussion Questions

1. "What was easy to communicate without words? Hard?"

2. "What part of your body did you use most?"

3. "Did you learn any ways to improve your nonverbal communications or to make your meaning clearer?"

4. "Did you find yourself exaggerating your usual expressions or adding new ones?"

Follow-up

The group may share their experiences in "I learned statements"; other students can respond to those statements. It may be fruitful to discuss the changes in content and communication that occurred as the group became more proficient at sending and receiving nonverbal messages. If some students consistently altered messages (e.g., made them silly, made them "safe"), discuss those patterns.

The I Witness Experiment

Procedure

Have the students sit in a circle. The group picks one person to be the "Guesser," who then leaves the group. While the "Guesser" is gone, one person is asked to be a "Leader." The "Leader" makes different nonverbal signs, such as clapping hands, snapping fingers, or yawning, which everyone imitates. The "Guesser" returns and tries to guess the identity of the "Leader." Several rounds can be played.

This exercise is designed to develop communication skills of attending and being aware of nonverbal behavior.

Discussion Question

1. "What did you do to enable you to guess the 'Leader'?"

2. "How well did you imitate the 'Leader'?"

3. "What things make it easy to imitate a person?"

4. "What makes it hard?"

I Witness is adapted from Allen Evey, Professor, University of Massachusetts.

Lesson 23: Rethinking Change

BEGINNING

Invite the group to share about deliberately making changes in life/behavior. Introduce the concept of communicating "here-and-now" feelings. "What kind of person would you be if you had no inner zone? How do you know what zone you are in?"

Review vocabulary: expectations, change, deliberate, fantasy.

ASSIGNMENT

Write down in your journal two changes you have deliberately made in your life and be prepared to share them with other members of the group.

AFFECTIVE EXPERIENCE

• The Animal Metaphor Fantasy Experience.

COGNITIVE INQUIRY

1. "Describe in your journal what happened and what you felt."

2. "Can you change how you felt or how you responded? How?"

3. "Have you ever changed your habits, behaviors or patterns in your life? What did you change? Why did you change? Did someone help you? Who? How? What are some of the things you would like to do differently in here? Who can help you?"

4. "Sometimes when people want to do something differently (like talking to someone new, trying a different way of talking to teachers, or asking for what you want), they convince themselves **not** to take the risk. When that happens to you, what is it that you are saying to yourself that stops you?"

USING YOUR ZONES

When you feel stuck in the inner zone of awareness, try naming your feelings to yourself, either inside or out loud. For example, if you're supposed to be studying your math, and you can't think because you are feeling sad about losing a friend, say just that to yourself, your classmate, or to the teacher.

When you are in an argument or feel one coming on, pay attention to what zone you're in. Win-lose arguments and fights usually happen to people who are in their middle zone. If, instead of staying in your awareness of your thoughts, plans, and expectations of others, you name the feelings you're having (inner zone), and what you are seeing and hearing in the other (outer zone), it will be difficult to keep the argument going. For example, when someone cuts in line in front of you, try saying, "I feel frustrated, having waited my turn and seeing you cut in line."

NOTES FROM KAREN'S JOURNAL

We asked the group to "Think of the person you like the most. Now think of an animal that's like that person."

Eric: Cat. My friend, Frank. He is twelve. He reminds me of a cat because he is nice.

Stuart: Deer. My girl friend. We play "Bambi" when we are together.

Katrina: Dog. My friend. She loves dogs. Wonderful!

Heidi: Horse. A horse is happy, nice. My friend, Kathy, who lives next door.

Let's think about all the words we know that relate to the person we like the most. "Happy; Great; Overjoyed; Good; Fun; Silly"

continues on page 73

PROCEDURE

"Imagine a huge forest. In the middle of it is a large open field. You are an animal walking toward the center of the field, and you see another animal that is the person you dislike the most."

Pause while the students imagine what happens and how they feel. "Now wipe the slate clean — that scene fades and suddenly the field appears in your mind again. This time as you approach the middle of the field you meet the animal that is the person you love most."

Pause for the children to imagine what happens. "When you're ready, return to this room and slowly open your eyes."

FOLLOW-UP

Immediately after the exercise, students should be given the opportunity to make an entry in their journals, describing in some detail what happened during the fantasy. Students should then be encouraged to share reactions with other members of the group and to consider a few questions, such as the following:

1. "How did you feel during each of the encounters?"

2. "Is this the way you usually react to these people?"

3. "What did you learn about yourself from your reactions?"

4. "How were your thoughts and feelings in both the first fantasy of this exercise and the last fantasy similar to, and different from, those of others?"

Finally students should be given the opportunity to make an additional entry in their journals, based on the questions and the group discussion.

The Animal Metaphor Fantasy

This exercise is relatively low in risk and is a good one for a transitional unit.

NOTES FROM KAREN'S JOURNAL, CONT.

Now let's make a list of words that might describe someone we do not like. "Sad; Bad; Angry; Hurt; Mad; Yucky; Cuckoo; Gooey"

Taylor: Ox. My neighbor is like an ox. He bothers everybody. Always runs into me.

Heidi: Lion. I do not like Scott. He is mean and sneaks up on me.

Eric: Cheetah. A boy named Miller, who lives down the street. He is really mean, and he never plays with me, and he can run fast.

"Now let's think of an animal that is most like you."

Katrina: Cat. Silly

Eric: Person. Energy, happy (sort of).

Stuart: Squirrel. Sometimes I feel small because I feel like I have no friends.

Taylor: I could not listen to Stuart because I was so anxious for my turn. That is what happens when you do not listen. That is bad. I get sent to my room; get sent home. If you do not listen, then, when it is your turn, they will not listen to you.

Heidi suggested we all brag [see The Bragging Experiment, page 99] about how we do not listen. We did. The group agreed we have a pattern of not listening.

We dealt with projections and got the group to think about the fact that they are responsible for their own reactions and responses.

LESSONS 24—29   # Approaching Goal 5

Disclosing Thoughts and Feelings

Lessons 24 through 29 further emphasize communication skills by helping the students feel comfortable about disclosing themselves; when it is appropriate, and when it is not, as well as how to encourage openness in others. Material dealt with so far is integrated and reviewed prior to completing the "Developing the Group" section of the course.

GROUP BEHAVIOR

Most self-disclosure at this point is external (i.e., outer zone). Usually children need considerable practice before they move into areas of personal concerns. Think of this Goal as seed-planting time. Results will come later in the course. You can contribute a great deal here by active role-modeling (i.e., demonstrating disclosure by discussion about yourself). Concentrate on the similarities within the group by reassuring and promoting a safe climate for disclosure, and permitting shy students to "pass" without fear of ridicule.

EVIDENCE OF AFFECTIVE GROWTH

* Showing an increasing ability to disclose thoughts and feelings.

* Showing an increasing ability to participate in self-disclosure exercises.

DISCUSSION QUESTIONS

Chat sessions on the importance of appropriate self-disclosure for its own sake and in support of the other class norms can be structured around the following kinds of questions and strategies.

1. "How appropriate is it to reveal or tell about yourself in here? Your real thoughts and feelings? Do you feel freer to disclose yourself somewhere else? What is different there? Do you learn anything by disclosing yourself?"

2. "People say if you keep your thoughts and feelings to yourself, you are better off. What do you think? When isn't that so?"

3. "Who can say what you are really thinking or feeling? Anyone? Many people?"

4. "When was a time you said more about yourself than you should have? When was a time you said less than you should have? What happened? What did you learn?"

5. "If others do not know what you feel, need or want, what do you lose by their not knowing? What do you avoid?"

EVIDENCE OF COGNITIVE GROWTH

* Classifying behavior into categories.

* Seeing patterns.

* Understanding the connection between behavior and communication.

* Valuing open communication.

* Conducting and reporting on experiments.

* Improving listening and question-asking skills.

BEGINNING

Ask students to sit in a circle. Discuss what has been learned so far in Self-Science. Discuss vocabulary: disclose, inner self, sender, receiver, pattern, consequences.

Lesson 24:
First Reactions

AFFECTIVE EXPERIENCE

- The Volunteer Experiment and the Rehearsing Experiment.

COGNITIVE INQUIRY

1. "How much do you reveal about yourself when you volunteer?"

2. "Are you affected by how much others disclose about themselves?"

3. See The Volunteer Experiment Trumpet Questions (page 76).

The Volunteer Experiment

PROCEDURE

1. Ask for volunteers to straighten up the room.

2. Ask for volunteers, but do not tell them the task, which could be to take notes for today's class.

Before the students do their tasks, ask the whole group to focus on their decision to volunteer or not to volunteer.

This exercise will help the students understand their feelings leading to the decision to volunteer or not to volunteer.

DISCUSSION QUESTIONS *(see page 76 for additional questions)*

1. "Were you affected by others' responses? How?"

2. "Were you concerned about how you might appear to your classmates or the teacher?"

3. "Did this concern affect your decision?"

4. "Can you state briefly how you decided to volunteer or not to volunteer?" (The answer to the last question might be shared with the entire class by several volunteers who wish to do so.)

5. "What pattern do you follow about volunteering? Are there certain conditions which let you volunteer?

FOLLOW-UP

Tell the class, "Close your eyes for a few minutes and see if you can play back that scene we just experienced. What were you feeling after I asked for volunteers? What questions were going on in your head? If you looked in a mirror, how would you look? What was your body saying? Was there a tightness anywhere?" After a few minutes, tell the group, "Open your eyes and write down in your journals anything you might have observed about yourself."

Have the class write journal entries in response to what was learned through the experiments and discussions.

The Volunteer Experiment Trumpet Questions

These questions help introduce the Trumpet Process by applying it to the Volunteer Experiment (page 75).

Either now, or at another time soon, you should provide another opportunity to volunteer.

FUNCTION

1. "Let's take a look at the patterns of those of you that volunteered."

2. "What does volunteering get for you in terms of outer feelings?" (e.g., attention, status, recognition.)

3. "What inner feelings does it give you?" (e.g., satisfaction.)

4. "Does it enable you to do something you want to do?"

5. "Is this your usual response, or pattern? If so, how does it make you feel that this is your usual pattern? If not, what was unusual about this situation that led you to your response?"

The same questions can be used for the students who don't usually volunteer. An additional question might be: "What does not volunteering protect you from or help you avoid?"

CONSEQUENCES

"What price do you pay for volunteering or not volunteering? How much does it cost? Are you losing out on anything? If so, what? If someone were thinking of adopting your pattern, what precautions might you give them?"

EVALUATION

"If you tried on an alternative behavior pattern, you might make a comparison with your first pattern. To help, you might complete the following statements: 'I learned . . .' 'I disliked/liked it because...'"

CHOOSE

After evaluating the alternative behavior and comparing it with the original pattern, the student can select either behavior or both as part of his/her repertoire.

The Rehearsing Experiment

This exercise is designed for use with other disclosure exercises. It increases the awareness of the process of rehearsing inner self-dialogues.

PROCEDURE

At any time when students are sharing responses, ask if anyone is "rehearsing" an answer. Ask for volunteers to share those inner self-dialogues.

FOLLOW-UP

Call attention to "rehearsing" by having a contest for the most responses (offer a prize). Give 30 seconds to name reasons for brushing teeth. Then give unlimited time to create the first line of a poem. Ask students to pay attention to inner dialogue and to note if they are thinking of more responses that they are sharing.

VARIATION

Ask a volunteer to role-play an inner dialogue, using a separate chair for each voice. Miming with words works well here.

BEGINNING

Ask students to share patterns identified in their journals. Review the concept of patterns.

Lesson 25: Sharing Yourself

AFFECTIVE EXPERIENCE

- The One Minute Autobiography Experiment.

- The Empty Your Wallet, Pockets, or Purses Experiment.

COGNITIVE INQUIRY

1. "How much were you willing to reveal about yourself?"

2. "Are you embarrassed to talk about yourself? Why?"

Have the class add "I learned..." statements to their journals.

ASSIGNMENT

Conduct two one-minute autobiography sessions with your friends and/or members of your family, and record notes about each in your journals. This assignment can come either before or after this lesson.

PROCEDURE

Divide the class into groups of five or six. Ask each child to think about his/her history from birth to the present. Tell the children that each will have one minute to relate personal autobiographies. Give children time to think. Then have them share their autobiographies orally in the small groups.

For the first run of this exercise the teacher should avoid modeling any particular style or theme of autobiography; this makes it easier for each child to express unique views. Sometimes children tend to copy each other's themes. For example, if one child describes personal experiences in terms of various medical operations, other children may follow, describing their lives with special emphasis on operations. Be alert to this possibility and note themes that emerge.

DISCUSSION QUESTIONS

1. "What thoughts did you censor (hold back) as you were saying your autobiography out loud?"

2. "Did you give a well-rounded picture of yourself or did you reveal only your good side?"

VARIATION

Since children like this exercise, you can repeat it periodically, having them do one-minute autobiographies around relevant themes such as: houses I have lived in; friends I have had; new toys I have received; etc.

The One-Minute Autobiography Experiment

This exercise will help students view their lives in a variety of ways they may not have considered before. It offers a chance to share views with others, to become more aware of their own pictures of self, and to share some of their patterns.

The Empty Your Wallet, Pockets, Or Purses Experiment

This exercise has many possibilities, depending on the students' interests and concerns. They may explore their own feelings about themselves and others, their values, and their willingness to share or disclose themselves.

VARIATION

The groups can also successfully be either dyad or larger support groups of eight or more, depending on the class.

PROCEDURE

Have groups of three to five students empty their pockets or wallets. Allow students to censor their items (to not share some items). Then each student can take a turn describing the contents of his/her wallet, purse or backpack. They can describe the person through the objects — "This person likes their family because they have lots of pictures of them...."

FOLLOW-UP

After the discussion, the teacher can ask the students to "be a detective" about themselves. Have the students write a list of the habits, likes, dislikes, and probable hopes or fears of "the suspect whose wallet this is." Each entry should have the supporting evidence listed from those items in the wallet or purse. Then, the group can be interrogated to see if the habits, etc. are consistent with those recognized by acquaintances. This is very helpful for the pattern clarification section of the Trumpet Process.

Journal entries, letters to the teacher, or further group sharing can include what the student hopes to have (or expects to have) in the purse or wallet one year from now, five years from now. Explore how each student is judging or evaluating him/herself based on what is not now in the purse or wallet. Anxieties about sharing, fantasies about what others are thinking about one's self, and how that makes one feel may also be appropriate here.

DISCUSSION QUESTIONS

1. "What are your feelings when you compare your items to other people's?"

2. "What are you censoring or not showing? What are you protecting by not showing it?"

3. "What feelings are you having about individual items of yours—sadness, pride, etc? Are you surprised by what others show?"

4. "How are the contents of your wallet/purse/backpack the same as the others? How are they different?"

5. "Do you have vivid memories associated with some of the things? What feelings did you have then? What are your feelings about that memory right now?"

ADDITIONAL DISCUSSION QUESTIONS

1. "What did you **say** to yourself immediately after I gave instructions? How did your feelings change during the activity? What was happening when they changed?"

2. "Did you make any discoveries during this activity?"

3. "What things would have made you feel better if they had been in your wallet or purse?"

4. "What will be in your pocket/purse/backpack when you are the person you want to be?"

BEGINNING

Discuss the homework assignment. Review terms: disclosure, self-description, intimates, acquaintances, concentric.

Lesson 26: Levels of Intimacy

AFFECTIVE EXPERIENCE

• The Privacy Blocks Experiment.

COGNITIVE INQUIRY

1. "Was the Privacy Blocks diagram helpful?"

2. "Would you change it in any way?"

3. "Are there some areas easier to disclose than others?"

4. "How much is it appropriate to reveal?"

5. "Can people be trusted with your real thoughts and feelings?"

6. "Do you learn anything by disclosing information about yourself?"

ASSIGNMENT

In your journal, make a list of at least two people for each of these categories: intimates, friends, acquaintances, everyone.

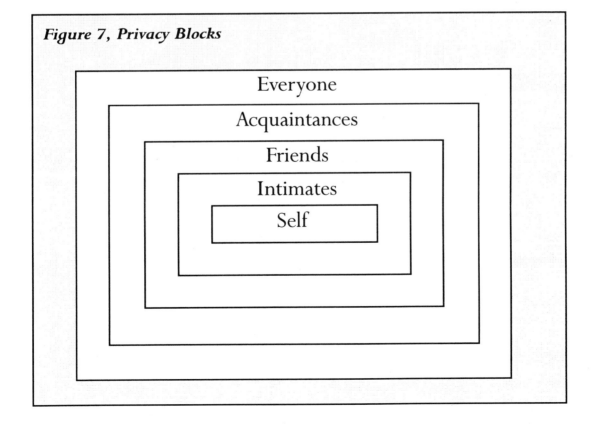

Figure 7, Privacy Blocks

Everyone

Acquaintances

Friends

Intimates

Self

The Privacy Blocks Experiment

This is an exercise to help students take a look at their patterns of disclosure. They will take a look at some of the criteria they use as individuals in deciding what things they talk about to whom.

PROCEDURE

Draw the diagram (Figure 7) from the last page on the board. Explain it:

The Privacy Blocks figure is a series of concentric squares dealing with what you disclose, and to whom. In the first square is self; it holds those things which you say to yourself. The next square, outside of that one, is for intimates, defined as one or two close friends, or members of the family. They are just the small number of people with whom you can share most of who you are. In the next square are friends, from school, from the community, and also including family members who are not as close as intimate ones. The next square is for acquaintances; classmates you really do not know very well, other students in the school that you meet, and neighbors a couple of doors down that you do not see very often. The final square includes absolutely everyone.

Ask the children to draw their own blocks; for each situation below, have them write the keyword in a block to show who they would tell.

situation	keyword to write
you hit a dog with your car and did not stop	DOG
you cheated on a test	CHEAT
you love someone	LOVE
you hate someone	HATE
you knew your best friend shoplifted	BEST FRIEND
you knew you only had six months to live	SIX MONTHS

DISCUSSION QUESTIONS

1. "What kinds of statements do you say to yourself that you can't share with anyone?"

2. "What kinds of statements can you share with your intimates, friends, and acquaintances?"

3. "What kinds of things can you share with acquaintances and not your intimates?"

4. "Do you find yourself keeping a lot of things to yourself?"

5. "Do you have confusion about what 'people' consider private?"

6. "How does it serve you to reveal certain things only to intimates, only to friends, only to acquaintances?"

7. "What are you protecting by keeping some things private?"

FOLLOW-UP

Write "I learned that I..." statements in journals, share them in dyads, or share in the whole group.

Lesson 27: Increasing Self-Disclosure

BEGINNING

Reflect on other self-disclosure activities you've done (like Privacy Blocks). Discuss the importance of understanding your own strengths — and how that is different from "bragging."

AFFECTIVE EXPERIENCE

• The Who Am I Experiment.

COGNITIVE INQUIRY

1. "What's the difference between self-disclosure and bragging?"

2. "Were your answers different than those you collected for homework? What does that tell you?"

3. "How honest were you? What would it have taken for you to be 100% honest? Is 100% honesty a reasonable goal?"

ASSIGNMENT

Ask three people to each give you one adjective to describe you; record the words in your journal.

The Who Am I Experiment

In this exercise students share elements of themselves. It can be used over longer periods of time to create great depth — and often with surprising recognition for students.

PROCEDURE

Divide the class into dyads. One person will be the active listener for one minute. S/he asks, "What are you good at?" The partner answers, over and over, each time beginning with, "I am good at..." Whenever the partner gets stuck, the listener asks again. Otherwise, the listener can not speak.

It is important to demonstrate this technique. When taken seriously it is remarkable.

DISCUSSION QUESTIONS

1. "Was it difficult to talk about yourself in this way? Was it enjoyable?"
2. "Did you like being told that it was okay to share this part of yourself?"
3. "Were there things that came to your mind that you decided not to share?"
4. "What was it like being listened too? Did you want your partner to talk more?"

OPTIONAL FOLLOW-UP

At the end of the five minutes, the class comes together as one group. Each student in turn tells about whom s/he talked with and shares one special thing about that person that seemed most important. Group sharing of feelings after talking to someone else about yourself can be preceded by some quiet reflections along that line in personal journals. Individuals can be asked to consider what they learned about the listening process while doing this exercise.

VARIATIONS

The listener can ask a range of questions from, "Who are you?" to "What are you afraid of?"

The time can be extended (even for several hours).

The listener can write down answers.

The subject can be "lighthearted" to build group connection and intimacy in a less bonded group; ask questions like, "What kind of television shows do you like?" In those cases, shorten the time for the dialogue.

Sometimes when there is a high level of trust between the partners, the listener can take a more active role and suggest answers.

Adapted from Barry Barankin and from Stephen K. Smuin.

Lesson 28: Nonverbal Disclosure

BEGINNING

Review the concentric square concepts and the relationships between friends, intimates, etc.

AFFECTIVE EXPERIENCE

- Complete the "Me" Picture Activity.

COGNITIVE INQUIRY

1. "Do the pictures of others match your feelings about them?"
2. "Are some congruent and others not? Why do you think this is so?"
3. "Can you tell from the pictures the things others like most about themselves?"
4. "Can you tell from the pictures the things others have the greatest concern about?"

ASSIGNMENT

Collect pictures from newspapers or magazines that remind you of yourself. Collect five very different images.

MATERIALS

crayons, butcher paper.

PROCEDURE

Instruct students to draw pictures of themselves as well as two things they think about frequently. While they are working, when you have finished your own picture, walk around and informally discuss pictures with the students. Listen to their conversations and observe. Have students share their pictures. Make it clear that this is voluntary. The sharer merely explains the picture to the group. Ask questions such as, "Will you tell us about this part of your picture? What feelings does this generate?"

DISCUSSION QUESTIONS

1. "The thing on my picture I think about most is..."
2. "There seems to be a pattern about my concerns which is..."

The "Me" Picture Activity

This exercise is to help students begin to: share facts about themselves, observe themselves, and share some of their concerns.

VARIATION

Ask the students to write explanations of their pictures and attach them. Put the explanations and pictures up on the wall someplace in the room. Have them share their pictures in quartets for about twenty minutes.

Have students draw similar pictures of the family and/or home.

Lesson 29: Disclosure and Intimacy

BEGINNING

Have a few students share their drawings about "teacher." The teacher then shares feelings about the things the students expressed. (This is an important time for the teacher to illustrate openness — with sincerity.)

Explain the "Here-and-Now" wheel concept (see pages 68, 69).

ASSIGNMENT

In your journal draw a picture of your teacher and show the things about which the teacher is happiest and the things about which the teacher has the most concern.

AFFECTIVE EXPERIENCE

- Public/Private Here-and-Now Wheels.

COGNITIVE INQUIRY

Ask questions associated with the private wheel. (Students need not share.) Ask questions associated with the public wheel. (Students share.)

1. "To whom can you say what you are really thinking or feeling? Anyone? Many people?"

2. "Are there times when people say more than they should about themselves? Have you?"

3. "Are there times when people say less than they should about themselves? Have you? What happened?"

4. "If others do not know what you feel, need, or want, what do you lose by their not knowing? What do you avoid?"

Public / Private Here-and-Now Wheels

PROCEDURE

Have the class do a private "Here-and-Now" wheel in their journals. See page 69 for an explanation and example Wheels.

Next have the class do a **public** "Here-and-Now" wheel to share with the group.

This exercise helps students examine their patterns of disclosure. It will help them look at the ways and reasons why they censor their feelings.

DISCUSSION QUESTIONS

1. "Is there a difference in the two wheels? What feelings do you find the hardest to share? Are there some feelings you can share with only certain people? Some useful open-ended sentences are: "I discovered that I ...," "I learned that I...," "I was surprised that I..."

FOLLOW-UP

In journals, dyads, or small groups, describe how you feel about each wheel.

Winding Up Goals 1-5

The lessons so far were designed to help the student become comfortable in the group; to permit the group process to develop to a middle "safe" stage. They also provided a structure of affective experience tied to cognitive inquiry. Learning has been primarily general and external—observing, identifying, classifying, and developing a mental framework for the study of self.

The next five lessons provide the cognitive framework within which the rest of the course will proceed. Students are already familiar with the first three steps of the Trumpet. Now they will learn the entire Trumpet pattern as a forerunner for applying the pattern to deeper studies of self.

Depending on the way you have scheduled the course, there may be a break after Lesson 34 (the end of the section). In any event, celebrate accomplishments thus far with a party, event, or field-trip to recognize growth and create a sense of closure.

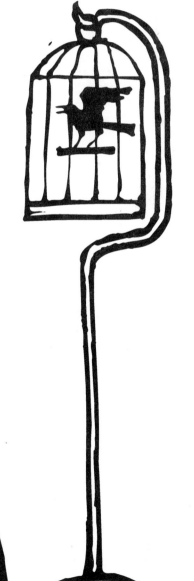

ANTICIPATED OUTCOMES

Students will learn an eight-step cognitive "road map" for charting affective experiences. An understanding of the Trumpet model is essential. The teacher may need to try a variety of approaches to help the student learn this new tool.

MATERIALS

For each of the following lessons the teacher is encouraged to have available (on display) the Trumpet diagram (see page 12). Students can quickly identify with the parts of the Trumpet that match the process they are learning.

Lesson 30: Introducing the Trumpet

BEGINNING

Put the Trumpet diagram up on one of the walls or draw the trumpet on the chalkboard. Ask what "share experiences" means. Review the term "inventory responses" (i.e., list, like a scientist, the "whats" — these can be feelings or bodily sensations, thoughts, and/or actions or behaviors).

Discuss the need for problem-solving skills.

ASSIGNMENT

Look over your journal for the past three weeks and see if you can write two paragraphs about things learned during that time.

MATERIALS

Picture book with a repeated conflict.

AFFECTIVE EXPERIENCE

- Read aloud a story like *Max's Dragon Shirt* by Rosemary Wells. (Older children like picture books too — as long as the teacher shares them in a 'grown-up' way.)

COGNITIVE INQUIRY

1. "What was the confrontation in the story?"

2 "What were the responses?" (create an inventory)

When inventorying responses we explore the WHAT? HOW? WHEN? WHERE? rather than the WHY?

3. "Are there reasons why different responses would be valuable?

4. Explain and discuss the Trumpet.

EXPLANATION OF THE TRUMPET PROCESS

Learning how to be a self-scientist is similar to learning how to play ball, solve math problems, etc. You need to have certain skills, to use a precise language (vocabulary), and to understand certain processes. You've already developed some skills, such as attending (i.e., paying attention, listening) to one another, keeping each other's trust, and so forth. You've also begun to learn a new language for talking about your thoughts, feelings, and actions. You have many of these new language words in your journal. Now, we will learn a process for studying ourselves. This process is called The Trumpet.

The Trumpet is an eight-step process, a road map — a set of guideposts — which can help us become self-scientists. It can help us better understand ourselves, how we relate to others, how we can be in control of our lives.

At this time we are our own textbooks. We are our own educators. We are the content, the material, of self-science because the subject of this course is each of us as people. As we begin at the narrow end of the Trumpet and proceed through the wide end, we will grow as people. For the next few lessons we will study each step of the Trumpet more carefully. The first two steps in the process are what we call "Share Experiences" and "Inventory Responses." These steps are illustrated on the Trumpet chart.

Lesson 31: Recognize & Own Patterns

BEGINNING

One helpful technique is to have students keep a running response inventory every time you do a consensus activity. Then, when you complete this activity, that collection of data may help them see their own patterns.

AFFECTIVE EXPERIENCE

• The Value Sort Experiment.

COGNITIVE INQUIRY

1. "How do you know when you are following a pattern?"

2. "How do your patterns help you? Do they hurt you too?"

3. "What does it mean to 'own' patterns? Is that hard? Why?"

The Value Sort Experiment

PROCEDURE

Copy the Value Sort cards (or make your own) and cut them up, one set for each student. Have them sort the cards from the one that is the very most important to the one that is the least important (but not necessarily unimportant or bad).

In groups of 5, have them lay out their cards in rows so everyone's #1 is on the far left and #8 is on the far right.

Next have the students in each group come to consensus and create one set.

Finally, have the whole class share their small-group sets, laying them out in rows as before, one group's row below the other.

DISCUSSION QUESTIONS

1. "Did you see a pattern to the choices? Were some values consistently high and others consistently low?"

2. "How did you feel about moving the cards for the consensus sort? Inventory your responses."

*This activity helps children see how their own points of view are like and unlike their peers. It shows a **literal** pattern, which can help explore the idea of internal patterns.*

Figure 8: Value Sort Cards

From Self-Science, McCown, Jensen et al. © 1998, Six Seconds.

The owner of this book has permission to duplicate this page for her or his own classroom.

BEGINNING

Discuss the homework and the idea that patterns have positive and negative results. Depending on the group, discuss the idea that patterns are developed because we want or need something. Ask someone to share her/his pattern and discuss the need it fills.

AFFECTIVE EXPERIENCE

- The 12 Sided Square Experience.

COGNITIVE INQUIRY

1. "Why do we follow patterns even when the consequences are negative?"

2. "What makes it easier / harder to allow alternatives?"

3. "What happens when someone else gives you alternatives? When your parent does? Your teacher? Your friend? Inventory your responses to each of those people when they give you alternatives. What does that inventory suggest?"

PROCEDURE

It is useful to have a few observers for this activity, particularly to keep group members from tripping or bumping. You can assign each observer to carefully watch a small number of participants.

Ask the participants to blindfold themselves — any size group is fine, 12 is manageable. The more people, the harder the challenge.

Ask the participants to stretch the entire rope into one large square with NO talking.

DISCUSSION QUESTIONS

Ask the observers to inventory what they saw.

1. "What was hard about this activity?" (we couldn't talk, we couldn't see)

2. "What was hard inside yourself?" (I was scared — of what?)

Lesson 32: Consider Consequences & Allow Alternatives

ASSIGNMENT

Identify three of your patterns. Make a list of how each helps you, and a list of how each hurts you.

MATERIALS

25' of cotton or nylon rope, around 1/2" in diameter

blindfolds for 12 people or half the group

The 12 Sided Square

This activity helps build group and it provides opportunities to see clear consequences and alternatives to behaviors.

VARIATIONS

Give permission for one person to talk. Pick someone who rarely talks, and rotate the responsibility.

Have the group make other figures; a circle, a triangle, even a star.

Lesson 33: Make Evaluations, Choose

BEGINNING

Current research shows that optimism leads to many positive results, and that it can be taught. One key difference between optimists and pessimists is that pessimists see failure as personal, permanent and pervasive. Optimists see the opposite about failure — but see success as personal, permanent, and pervasive.

Share these findings with your students and discuss the outcomes of optimism.

ASSIGNMENT

Observe yourself for one day, and note your reactions in terms of being optimistic or pessimistic.

AFFECTIVE EXPERIENCE

- Complete the Optimism Graphs and discuss.

COGNITIVE INQUIRY

1. "Research says optimism is something people can learn. What do you think?"
2. "If you could learn to be more optimistic, how would you learn it?"
3. "What are the consequences of being optimistic?"
4. "Some people say that 'not choosing is a choice.' Do you agree? What does that mean in terms of your own patterns?"

MATERIALS

Optimism Graphs, one per student

Optimism Graphs

Positive Event:		
	Optimistic View	Pessimistic View
Who's fault/responsibility is it?		
How long will it last?		
How big a "deal" is it?		

Negative Event:		
	Optimistic View	Pessimistic View
Who's fault/responsibility is it?		
How long will it last?		
How big a "deal" is it?		

From Self-Science, McCown, Jensen et al. © 1998, Six Seconds.
The owner of this book has permission to duplicate this page for her or his own classroom.

BEGINNING

Review the journal assignment, and discuss how the Trumpet can be used in everyday life.

Lesson 34: Trumpet Summary

AFFECTIVE EXPERIENCE

- Review and discuss the Trumpet Scenarios.

COGNITIVE INQUIRY

1. "Is it easier to use the Trumpet on yourself or on someone else?"

2. "What is the difference between recognizing one of your patterns and blaming yourself?"

3. "What happens if new choices lead to new confrontations?"

4. "Is conflict bad?"

ASSIGNMENT

Create your own metaphor for the 8 steps of the Trumpet process.

MATERIALS

Copies of Trumpet Scenarios

SITUATION: DAVID LAUGHS

David is in the fourth grade, the unannounced leader of the boys. In many ways he has instigated ridicule and laughter among the boys toward the girls of the class. But the girls are aware of the situation and confront David by telling him how his behavior makes them feel. David's response is, "Tough! It makes me feel good."

SHARE EXPERIENCES

How do you think David feels?

What sentences do you think he was saying to himself?

How do you think he is affected by the response of others?

How might his face and body look as he says the above quote?

OWN PATTERNS

Can you think of anything he gets out of being the way he is? Try to list five things he gets from his actions.

CONSEQUENCES

If you were David, would you be missing out on anything? When you ridicule someone, what price do you pay?

IDENTIFY PATTERNS

See if you can think of several patterns for David. What are they? How would you describe the typical David?

ALTERNATIVES

What other alternatives could David choose?

Trumpet Scenarios

Each of these situations is followed by a series of questions in order of the Trumpet. You can read these aloud and discuss them as a whole group, or you can copy them and process them in small groups.

From Self-Science, McCown, Jensen et al. © 1998, Six Seconds.
The owner of this book has permission to duplicate this page for her or his own classroom.

SITUATION: LOUISE DOESN'T CARE

Louise is an honor student, has been since sixth grade. Now in the tenth grade she has lost interest in school, studies, and friends. Most of her evenings she spends in her room reading. On weekends she seldom joins the crowd for any fun. Last year her father and mother decided to get a divorce after years of family conflict. When called in by the counselor about her grades, the counselor inquired, "Can you tell me what's bothering you?" Louise responded, "What difference does it make?"

SHARE EXPERIENCES

Imagine you are Louise. What is she feeling? Try to look like Louise looks. If you had to choose one word to describe her, what would it be?

IDENTIFY AND OWN PATTERNS

Name Louise's pattern. What does Louise get from her pattern? What need does she satisfy?

"How does Louise's indifference help her? Why would this attitude help her deal with her situation?"

CONSEQUENCE

"What is Louise avoiding? Or protecting? Is she missing out on anything?"

ALTERNATIVE

"If you were Louise, what other things could you say to the counselor? What are the first steps you would take, if you were Louise, to change?"

EVALUATION

"If you were Louise, what would be the most scary part about making a change?"

SITUATION: TIM'S FIRST DAY

Tim just moved to a new community He knew none of his fellow students in the second grade. When his dad took him to school the first day, Tim started to cry.

SHARE EXPERIENCES

"If you were Tim, describe the feelings you would have. Are you more concerned with yourself or how others view you? When have you responded in a similar fashion?"

PATTERNS

"In what kind of setting do you respond as Tim did? Are these settings similar in any way?"

OWN PATTERNS

"If this is your pattern, what do you get out of it? What do people do to or for you when you cry?"

CONSEQUENCE

"What is the result of your behavior in a similar setting?"

ALTERNATIVE

"What are some different endings to this story?"

"What has to happen for these new endings to be real?"

From Self-Science, McCown, Jensen et al. © 1998, Six Seconds.
The owner of this book has permission to duplicate this page for her or his own classroom.

SITUATION: SUE IS LATE

Sue has come late to spelling class five days in a row. The lingering in the halls is due to her involvement with Armando at the lockers. Finally the teacher asks her to stay after class to speak to her about her tardiness. From the back of the room George calls out, "You'd better get Armando in, too." Sue blushes.

SHARE EXPERIENCES

How do you think Sue feels, George feels, and the teacher feels? Who is most comfortable? Least comfortable?

OWN PATTERNS

Obviously Sue is getting something out of being late. What might make it worth her being late for class? Can you relate this to your life?

PATTERNS

Is there any part of the story which surprised you? If you were Sue, how would you have responded?

CONSEQUENCE

Think of a similar situation in your life and remind yourself what you have done, how you have acted. Are you willing to share your experiences with the rest of us?

SITUATION: FOOTBALL PRESSURE

The football team has had a 4-0 season so far. The coach is putting more and more pressure on the team to practice, keep curfew and be on time. Finally one of them speaks up and complains about the price they have to pay to be on the team: "I'm quitting unless the pressure starts cooling off." The others chime in, "Right on!"

SHARE EXPERIENCES

How do you think the team felt right after the one team member spoke up? What sentences would you be saying to yourself if you were them?

CONSEQUENCE

What are the team members willing to take? Are they missing out on anything? What precautions must they consider?

IDENTIFY AND OWN PATTERNS

What patterns do you see in the situation? Think of the time you spoke up and how you felt about it.

What will the team gain by going along with or by opposing the coach? What will the coach gain by pressuring the team or by not pressuring the team?

ALTERNATIVES

What alternatives are open to members of the team?

EVALUATION

What ending to the story would you choose?

*From Self-Science, McCown, Jensen et al. © 1998, Six Seconds.
The owner of this book has permission to duplicate this page for her or his own classroom.*

Section 3
Developing Accountability

You may have new students in your class now, you may be returning from a vacation, or you may simply feel the need to review before moving on. In these cases, take time to return to earlier lessons on naming feelings, inventorying, and building trust in the group.

This second half of the course moves from self-knowledge to self-choice. The first half of the course provided critical skills; this half provides an opportunity to use those skills.

Many students will not reach the goals of this half of the course. They will resist the fact that they have choice about their own feelings. Many students will not accept, initially, that they are accountable. It is actually easier to let other people be in charge, to blame, to criticize. So, don't be frustrated if the message doesn't "stick" the first time... or the fiftieth — it is still valuable and still worth the effort. You are planting seeds now; seeds that might not bloom this year, but the harvest is worth the wait.

Approaching Goal 6

Enhancing Self-Esteem in Terms of Awareness and Accepting One's Strengths

Lessons 35 through 37 build the foundation for the harder work in self-exploration which follows. It is impossible to "dig" for weaknesses and self-improvement without a sense of where one's strengths are. We too often harp and nag and chide on weaknesses, ignoring the very real need to feel pride before permitting criticism (from self or others).

GROUP BEHAVIOR

Some students have a harder time than others in celebrating, bragging or just talking about their strengths and accomplishments. Certain myths in our culture about "humility" cause confusion about personal worth; this must be addressed. It is not enough to simply ask children to feel good about themselves; the challenge is to build recognition of **real** accomplishments and strengths. The experiences in this section can lead to tremendous growth when pride is clarified and sanctioned.

EVIDENCE OF AFFECTIVE GROWTH

- Thinking and feeling more positively about self.
- Liking self.
- Laughing at self.
- Expressing pride in self.
- Describing personal strengths and weaknesses with greater accuracy.

EVIDENCE OF COGNITIVE GROWTH

- Learning to make evaluations and judgments.
- Relating ethical concepts to characters in fiction and myths.
- Reinforcing skills in classifying data.

NOTES ON ESTEEM FOR LESSONS 35 AND 36

Enhancing a student's self-esteem isn't easy. Frequently a student's self-esteem is intimately related to academic performance. Needless to say, there isn't a one-to-one relationship between self-esteem and academic performance. This happens both because the term is vague and because of people's general difficulty in accurately assessing their own self-esteem.

Many students, when beginning a new class, want to impress the teacher with their self-confidence and abilities; consequently, measuring self-esteem during the initial phases of a Self-Science class often yields an inflated measure. As the year progresses, however, students realize their Self-Science class is a safe place to admit weaknesses as well as to accentu-

continues, top of page 97

ate strengths. A more accurate measure of self-esteem can be obtained midway through the year.

Discussions at this point can be focused on the following kinds of questions. Is it important to know what you can do well and what you can't? Where is it safe to talk about these things? Do you have to be good at everything? What are the ways others can make you feel good about yourself? What are the ways you can make yourself feel good about yourself? Is there a difference between accentuating/celebrating your strengths and bragging? What are the differences?

Such discussions provide a basis for students to both assess their own capabilities and potentials, and to distinguish these qualities from their own self-worth. As students become more familiar with their many and varied strengths and weaknesses, they generally develop a more trusting attitude toward their own capabilities as well as toward other members of the class. They start to discover that even the "smartest" and most popular students have weaknesses, and that those who are struggling or less popular have strengths. This attitude allows students to begin feeling better about themselves; they are able to begin developing foundations for accepting responsibility for personal thoughts, feelings, and actions.

RE-OWNING

After a brief description and modeling by the teacher, students will quickly understand the concept of "re-owning."

"Re-owning" means repeating what has been said about someone or something else as though it were descriptive of yourself. For example, if a student chooses an animal like a dog and states that a dog is kind, the "re-owning" process would be to have the student say, "I am kind." Some projections are appropriate when "re-owned" and some are not.

A brief illustration enables students to decide for themselves when a projection is appropriate to "re-own." **One word of caution:** students shouldn't be forced when dealing with a highly negative projection. Under these circumstances, simply let the student address the **prospect** of re-owning. It is not necessary for her/him to say to everyone, "Yes, this is accurate for me."

Lesson 35: Re-own

MATERIALS

student contract forms, list of Self-Science goals, paper and pencils

BEGINNING

Review the first five goals of the Self-Science curriculum. Ask the children to give you feedback on what they've absorbed and understood about the goals. What was worth learning? What could be done to make it better?

Talk briefly about Goals 6 through 10. Explain what will be covered in Self-Science during the remaining class meetings. Ask for questions. Since the children have signed a Self-Science contract before, have a brief conversation about the need for commitment to the group in order to effectively participate in Self-Science. Ask each child to sign a new personal contract.

AFFECTIVE EXPERIENCE

- Distribute paper and pencils and explain the Animal Projection Experiment.

COGNITIVE INQUIRY

Discuss what "projection" means.

Discuss the term "re-own." (See page 97.)

1. "Was there at least one projection that you re-owned?"

2. "How did you feel when you were re-owning your projections?"

3. "What were you thinking? What were you doing?"

4. "What are some lessons from today? Where else could you use them?"

The Animal Projection Experiment

This exercise is particularly useful because of its flexibility. This exercise enhances learners' self-concepts and self-disclosures by increasing awareness of strengths and weaknesses.

PROCEDURE

When using this exercise for self-esteem, have students choose their favorite animal or the animal they would most like to be. Have the students write down the name of their animal and three positive qualities or characteristics of the animal. Students may then act out the qualities nonverbally or share them verbally with the group.

ALTERNATE PROCEDURE

Tell the class to choose the animal they like least, are afraid of, etc. Then have the students identify three positive and three negative qualities of the animal.

DISCUSSION ITEMS

Share the qualities chosen with the whole group. Ask the students to "re-own" the qualities for themselves. (See page 97 for a description of re-owning.)

Lesson 36: See Strengths

BEGINNING

(See notes on Esteem and Re-owning, pages 96 and 97.) Review the assignment and ask the group to explain the source of self-esteem.

AFFECTIVE EXPERIENCE

- Introduce the Bragging Experiment.
- Introduce the Pride Line Experiment.

COGNITIVE INQUIRY

1. "Is it easier to talk about strengths than weaknesses?"

2. "Do most people focus on strengths or weaknesses?"

3. "How do people feel when they hear only negative comments?"

ASSIGNMENT

In your journal list three qualities you really like about your best friend. Re-own them for yourself.

MATERIALS

pencil and paper (for each student)

The Bragging Experiment

PROCEDURE

Ask students to form groups of five or six. Instruct them that they have a total of fifteen to twenty minutes in which to brag and boast about anything they can think of.

DISCUSSION QUESTIONS

Ask the students to make journal entries regarding their feelings about bragging, and then ask the following questions.

1. "Did you enjoy it?"

2. "Were you uncomfortable?"

3. "How did you feel when others were bragging?"

4. "Did you feel competitive?"

5. "Did you want to make 'killer statements' to different people in the group? To whom? What brought on those feelings?"

VARIATION

Each member of the group writes three things s/he has done well and later shares them. The class sits in a circle and everyone completes the sentence, "I'm proud of..."

This exercise is useful for enhancing learners' self-concepts, for helping them feel more comfortable about acknowledging their own strengths and abilities, and for increasing rapport and self-disclosure.

The Pride Line Experiment

This exercise is used to enhance positive self-concept, to identify values in regard to action, and to increase self-disclosure.

PROCEDURE

Ask the students to make a statement about a specific item, beginning with, "I'm proud that...." For example, you might say, "I'd like you to mention something about your work in school that you're proud of. Please begin your response with, 'I'm proud that....'" Students may say, "I pass," if they wish.

DISCUSSION QUESTIONS

1. "How did you feel when you gave your 'Pride Line'?"

2. "Was there anything you wanted to say yet censored? What?"

VARIATIONS

Below are some suggested items for use in the Pride Line.

Things you've done for your parents.

Things you've done for a friend.

Things you've done for yourself.

Something you've done to fight pollution.

Something you've done athletically.

Something which you worked toward but have not yet achieved.

The Strength Bombardment Experiment

This exercise helps students gain a clearer recognition and overview of their strengths, personality resources, and capacities.

PROCEDURE

1. Brainstorm a list of personality strengths; write them on the board or on newsprint. To "prime the pump" the teacher may start by giving a couple of examples.

2. In small groups, one person at a time is the focus for the brainstorming of positive qualities. The other group members "bombard" him/her with all the strengths they see in him/her. The person being bombarded should remain silent until the group has finished. One member of the group should act as recorder, listing the strengths and giving them to the person when the group has finished. It may be necessary to caution the students that no "put-down" statements or "backhanded compliments" are allowed. This is a time to share only positives.

VARIATIONS

If the teacher wishes to continue the exercise further, the group fantasy strategy can be used. After the list of strengths has been completed, the teacher asks, "How would you see *Name of Student* functioning five years from now if s/he used all the strengths and potentialities?" The group then shares their fantasies and dreams about the chosen person.

Student can consider, "What is your own dream for yourself?" An additional follow-up activity is to have the students ask their parents to list strengths and then to add these strengths to the list collected in class. Other teachers could be solicited for comments as well.

DISCUSSION QUESTIONS

1. "How did you feel while this process was happening?"

2. "Were you surprised at any of the strengths you heard?"

3. "Do you consider any of the strengths you heard about yourself to be weaknesses?"

BEGINNING
Review assignment. Discuss concepts of: censorship, symbols, self-esteem, bragging, projections, owning, fantasy, self-disclosure.

Lesson 37: Support and Criticism

AFFECTIVE EXPERIENCE
- Introduce Strength Bombardment Experiment.
- Introduce Success Symbols Experiment.

ASSIGNMENT
Write in your journal five things you feel are positive about your teacher and five weaknesses.

COGNITIVE INQUIRY
1. "Are we more prone to criticize than to support people?"
2. "What price do we pay when we are critical?"
3. "What do we gain when we are positive? Lose?"

MATERIALS
newsprint, felt pens

PROCEDURE
Have the students imagine one or more tangible object(s) that recall or symbolize some past success or accomplishment they've had. During the class period have each student share one or more of the "success symbols" either with the rest of the class or with a small group. Instruct the students to share the feeling and meaning connected with the specific object as well as the success it symbolizes.

The Success Symbols Experiment

ACTIVITY
Ask students to make journal entries regarding their feelings before, during, and after the sharing of their success symbols.

DISCUSSION QUESTIONS
1. "What sentences were you saying to yourself when others were sharing?"
2. "As I was sharing, I noticed ...." "What I liked best was...."

VARIATIONS
Invite students to bring in object(s) that symbolize success. You can also ask them to bring objects that symbolize family, friendship, fear, or any other concept, experience, or emotion.

This exercise is used to enhance the learner's positive self-concept and to increase rapport and self-disclosure.

Approaching Goal 7

Accepting Responsibility

Lessons 38 to 41 explore some of the dynamics behind taking responsibility, "owning" one's feelings, thoughts, and actions. Students survey their own study habits (applying the Trumpet concepts) to encourage experience and responsibility in evaluating important areas of student life.

GROUP BEHAVIOR

For this Goal, you'll "peel the onion" of accountability another layer. These lessons promote awareness of how people project in order to avoid taking responsibility. Here you will have to move carefully, letting the awareness come out as students are able. Danger here is one of moralizing (i.e., "Stand on your own two feet"; "Who's to blame?"; "Did you do this?")

EVIDENCE OF AFFECTIVE GROWTH

* Gaining an increasing acceptance of feelings, moods, conduct, and the consequences of personal behavior.
* Gaining an increasing ability to follow through on a commitment.

EVIDENCE OF COGNITIVE GROWTH

* Beginning to understand the concepts of projection and avoidance.
* Applying evaluation skills to personal study habits.

Learning to accept responsibility for one's self is a lifelong task. The difficulty becomes evident when we see the two-year-old child with cookie crumbs on his/her face deny having eaten a cookie, or the adolescent student who proclaims the stupidity of the teacher when the student has just failed an exam, or the driver who blames his passenger's talking for the car accident, etc. We can all think of times when we have been either on the giving or the receiving end of similar situations.

A major impediment to accepting responsibility for self is the tendency to blame someone else for a given action. This cycle of blaming others and becoming a victim can be avoided by having each person accept responsibility for his/her own behavior. To be sure, there are many situations and social issues over which we have little control. We do, however, control our own **reactions**, so we have to accept responsibility for them. In the situation where the driver blames the accident on the chatty passenger, for example, it isn't so much the chatting which caused the accident but the driver's reaction (in this case attending to the words, not the road). **Being able to accept responsibility for self also allows others to accept responsibility for themselves,** ultimately decreasing the need to establish fault.

Discussion about accepting responsibility can revolve around such questions as: "Is it hard to admit something when you are wrong? Do others seem to have control over you? Does anyone ever really make you do something? How do these situations make you feel?"

Lesson 38: Who Makes Choices?

BEGINNING

Introduce the ideas of accepting responsibility and why all of us must accept responsibility for our own actions. Review the "alternatives" and "choosing" steps in the Trumpet.

AFFECTIVE EXPERIENCE

- The Robot Experiment
- Introduce the Time Diary Experiment

MATERIALS

Time Diary sheets for each student (see page 104).

COGNITIVE INQUIRY

Introduce the Time Diary Experiment. This experiment is an assignment for the students to keep a time-and-pattern diary of study habits over the next week. The purpose of the study is to demonstrate responsibility in a relevant form (i.e., each person is clearly responsible for his/her own studying).

The Robot Experiment

PROCEDURE

Students are requested to become robots with you as their master. They move in a stiff manner, follow your every command, doing only what they are programmed to do. Give them a series of repetitious, boring commands, such as requesting they take a step back and a step to the left when they bump into another person or object. Give some commands they can't possibly do; then chastise them for their inability to follow orders. Don't stop the exercise until some of the class is upset with following commands.

FOLLOW-UP

Have the class do a Here-and-Now Wheel, journal entries, or a group discussion of process questions.

DISCUSSION QUESTIONS

1. "What feelings are expressed in the Here-and-Now Wheel (see page 69)?"
2. "Do you ever feel like a robot? When?"
3. "Who are your masters?"
4. "What do you like and/or dislike about being a robot?"
5. "Do you feel trapped?"
6. "How much freedom did you feel you had to untrap yourself?"

This exercise is useful for gathering data about how students feel about following orders and a lack of choice. Discussion and/or groundrules about structure and freedom can evolve from this exercise.

Time Diary Experiment

Each person with a sense of responsibility has power over his/her actions. By studying one's behavior, one is able to consider alternatives for improvement and making choices. (This is a good opportunity for the teacher to use personal examples in keeping with the adult modeling role.)

PROCEDURE

Draw a week-long time-diary on the board with columns for "time used" and "time wasted." Together, fill in the diary for the day up to the time Self-Science class meets.

DISCUSSION QUESTIONS

The personal time diary should be discussed each class meeting to help the students think through their personal records. Ask these questions.

1. "What situation arose which caused time to be wasted?"

2. "Was this in keeping with your usual pattern?"

3. "What did you gain from your pattern?"

4. "Did you miss out on anything?"

5. "What alternatives might you choose?"

6. "What would you gain?"

7. "What would you lose?"

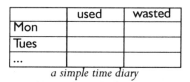

	used	wasted
Mon		
Tues		
...		

a simple time diary

NOTES FROM KAREN'S JOURNAL

The class looked at last week's videotape on the birthday party. There was a lot of giggling and embarrassment. They all shared their feelings about seeing themselves and there was general agreement that they did not recognize their own voices.

Then we played the Robot Game.

First we played it as a whole group and then in dyads. This group really enjoyed the game and had a very good discussion. Peter feels like a robot at home because of the way his older brothers and sisters treat him. He was able to go into detail and really get in touch with his resentment, which is important as he's always trying to live up to his image of his family.

George, on the other hand, doesn't feel like a robot but thought about his brother, whom he treats as if he were one. He decided his brother must not like it very much, and he would try to treat him differently.

The group generally related robot feelings to home where they felt they were being bossed around.

Again, today, the boys were particularly energetic when the group began. The whole group was talking and didn't stop even though I said we wouldn't be able to do any activities until they settled down. I waited about ten minutes, and then I had everyone "Freeze." I let them choose between staying frozen or sitting while we talked for a few minutes about why they came to Self-Science.

They responded: "To learn about ourselves." "To learn about others." "To learn about our feelings."

"How do we do this?" "Experiments." "Asking questions."

I felt a great deal of frustration dealing with the group today. On one hand I'd like to just let them go until they take control, but I don't feel that it's fair to the other children who want to do other things.

Lesson 39: Personal Power

BEGINNING

Introduce the concepts and vocabulary words of "approach" and "avoidance." ("Approach" is moving ahead or taking action; "avoidance" is keeping away from, or ignoring, or disliking certain actions.) People who approach a source of conflict, for example, may be working toward resolution.

AFFECTIVE EXPERIENCE

- The Power Continuum Experience.

COGNITIVE INQUIRY

1. "How much power do you have over your own actions?"

2. "Do people always think before they talk? Act? Do you?"

3. "What are some lessons from today? Where else could you use them?"

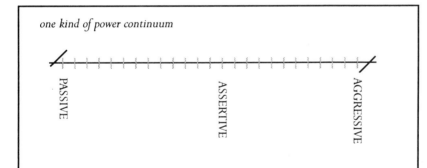

one kind of power continuum

PASSIVE   ASSERTIVE   AGGRESSIVE

ASSIGNMENT

Have the students each maintain an approach/avoidance diary for a week. Each day, they should write an example of a situation/conflict/issue/person they either avoided or approached.

MATERIALS

Power Continuum (one for each student)

The Power Continuum Experience

This exercise is designed to help kids see how to be assertive in a positive, clear manner.

PROCEDURE

Draw a continuum from "passive" to "assertive" to "aggressive."

Brainstorm examples of each behavior. Ask students for "real-life" examples without anyone's names.

Choose one example and role play. Act out the same situation three times, once with the "main character" being passive, once assertive, and once aggressive.

FOLLOW-UP

Have the group go stand on the continuum where they feel they are right now. Then move to where they feel they are most of the time. Finally, have them move to where they would like to be for the next week.

Ask students to copy the continuum into their journals, then mark the places where they stood.

DISCUSSION QUESTIONS

1. "What's positive or negative about the positions you marked?"

2. "Is there a difference between your actual position on the continuum and your desired position?"

3. "If there is a difference, what stops you from getting to your desired position?"

4. "Imagine a time when you have acted in your actual positions. How did you feel then?"

5. "Have you ever acted in your desired position? How did that feel?"

VARIATIONS

You can create a different continuum and use the same approach — elicit examples then have students physically move. It is important to acknowledge that we each fit in many places on the continuum depending on the situation.

Try creating a continuum outside with a long (50 foot) rope. You can mark many points, like a scale from one to ten, by tying strips of fabric to the rope.

BEGINNING

Review the idea that we have choice and responsibility for our actions.
Discuss the different kinds of choices we have.

Lesson 40:
Managing
Time

AFFECTIVE EXPERIENCE

- Share Time Diaries.

ASSIGNMENT

Continue your time diary (see page 104) for another week. On two days, see if you have the personal power to waste thirty minutes less time than for the same days the preceding week.

COGNITIVE INQUIRY

1. "What does your diary suggest about your use of time? Do you notice any patterns? What kinds? Is there anyone else who helps you waste time? Does it occur at any regular times?"

2. "Are you responsible for yourself?"

3. "Are you responsible for others?"

4. "Are you willing to process (out loud) your wasted time through the 'Trumpet'?"

5. "Are there any group patterns similar to individual patterns? How is this possible?"

6. "Are there any times during the day when more people seem to waste time than at others?"

MATERIALS

Time Diaries created in Lesson 38

Lesson 41: Projections

BEGINNING

Review concept of "projections."

AFFECTIVE EXPERIENCE

• Give the Teacher a Voice Experiment.

COGNITIVE INQUIRY

Have individuals act as teacher and have the children do their projections out loud and continue discussion questions.

Give The Teacher A Voice Experiment

PROCEDURE

Have the children look at you. Say, "I am going to sit here. I want you to imagine what I might be saying if I were to talk. Give me a voice; make it sound the way you think I would sound."

FOLLOW-UP

Make journal entries on the following questions.

1. "How did it feel to be my voice?"

2. "Did you think of things for my voice that you did not say?"

3. "If so, what kept you from saying them?"

This exercise is designed to get at students' subtle concerns through projection.

VARIATIONS

Have the children write their answers in their journals instead of giving them aloud.

Approaching Goal 8

Becoming Aware of Major Concerns

GROUP BEHAVIOR

The work in this Goal is a "cleansing" action. Students use the skills and concepts they have learned to focus on deep-seated concerns/issues. The ability to do this creates an internal freeing-up, a release, a letting-go. It takes much energy to keep fears and concerns inside. Obviously, some students will participate more deeply than others. Again, the seed-planting concept functions. Accept the group on whatever level they can reach.

EVIDENCE OF AFFECTIVE GROWTH

- An increasing ability to state specific personal concerns and relate personally to the concerns of others.

EVIDENCE OF COGNITIVE GROWTH

- Integrating and using the skills developed so far.

Lessons 42 through 44 use all the cognitive steps of the Trumpet to understand personal concerns and the validity of the concerns. This is, in effect, final preparation for the "payoff" of Self-Science — feeling free to examine and make changes in any one of a number of behavioral patterns.

It may seem unusual to think a person is unaware of personal concerns but, in fact, it is common. It's generally easier to be aware of external concerns than internal concerns. For example, a student may be aware of concerns over performance on an examination, but unaware of concerns about his ability to be a good friend. While some students may become aware of their concerns, there are few opportunities to express these concerns in an open, trusting environment. Some students have the advantage of being able to express concerns to their parents.

Self-Science class can provide students with a place they can safely and constructively express both their external and internal concerns. Through the gradual establishment of the norms and goals of the curriculum, a feeling of trust and safety is established. By acknowledging student input on all levels from the beginning of the year, students learn that discussing their concerns has validity.

Discussion can be focused around the following kinds of questions: "Have you ever felt as if you were the only person to be concerned about being alone? Do others usually relate their concerns to you? What are the situations that allow this to happen? To whom do you feel you can tell your concerns?"

Experiential activities about concerns help students realize that their fears and concerns are usually shared by peers. This facilitates their recognition of others' concerns, as well as accepting the responsibility for their own. Becoming more aware of personal concerns prepares students for recognizing their typical reactions and behavior patterns.

Lesson 42: Concerns and Fears

BEGINNING

Introduce the concept of "concerns for fears." (See notes in box, page 109.)

ASSIGNMENT

Write in your journal four fears you have; two you'd share and two you'd keep to yourself.

MATERIALS

3 x 5 cards (two for each student)

AFFECTIVE EXPERIENCE

- Secret in the Hat Experiment.
- Fear in the Hat Experiment.

COGNITIVE INQUIRY

1. "What other secrets/fears could you have given?"
2. "Is it too risky to give all your secrets/fears?"
3. "Did you keep some secrets/fears to yourself?"
4. "When people disclose themselves, is this a sign of weakness?"
5. "Is it easier to disclose yourself in this class?"
6. "Are there other places where you would feel free to disclose your secrets/fears ?"
7. "Why do secrets/fears exist? What would happen if we did not have any?"

PROCEDURE

Have students write a secret they've never told anyone on a 3 x 5 card and put it in the hat. There should be no names on the cards. Stir the cards and have each child select one card to read aloud and discuss.

VARIATION

Have students write fears on a card with their name. Then group students by similar fears and give them time to discuss their shared fears.

DISCUSSION QUESTIONS

1. "How did you feel hearing others' secrets?"

2. "How did you feel hearing your secret read?"

3. "How do you suppose the others felt?"

4. "Were you surprised to learn others had fears similar to your own?"

5. "How risky was it to disclose your fears?"

Secret in the Hat Experiment

This exercise is designed to identify concerns and to promote self-awareness.

INTRODUCTION

Before beginning, restate the necessity for taking the fear seriously. When students participate in this experiment for the first time, the fears presented are usually external, such as fear of the dark, snakes, etc. Gradually students move toward more internal concerns such as fear of not having a friend, being alone, etc. It is important that the teacher participate. This provides safety for the students as well as providing the teacher with the opportunity to subtly move the discussion of fears from external to internal.

PROCEDURE

Ask each child to write a fear on a 3 x 5 card and put it in the hat. Stir the cards and have each child select one from the hat. Have the students read the cards, one at a time.

FOLLOW-UP

After reading it, the child can speak to the card and tell it why s/he is not afraid of it.

DISCUSSION QUESTIONS

1. "How did you feel seeing someone else work on your fear?"

2. "How did you feel hearing others' fears?"

3. "Did you notice any patterns?"

4. "Has anyone else ever experienced the same or a similar kind of fear?"

5. "When are you most likely to experience such a fear?"

6. "Wouldn't most people experience that fear under similar circumstances?"

Fear in the Hat Experiment

This exercise is designed to clarify students' concerns and to promote self-awareness. It's particularly useful because it permits anonymity; students consequently are free to reveal as much or as little as they wish.

Notes from Karen's Journal

Today we introduced a new game, Fear in the Hat. The children decided to nonverbally act out the card they drew as a charade-like activity. After each fear was guessed or read, everyone added to the experience by relating to the particular fear. Everyone was willing to admit a fear to the group and to explain why. We talked about how we felt revealing our fears, learning about other peoples' and in the discussion recognized several patterns. One was a fear that related to a similar, real-life experience in the past. The other was fear for our safety and well-being.

Camille could not think of anything she was afraid of at first. She finally thought of something as I sat by her and discussed possibilities (e.g., being alone, scary noises, people fighting, getting hurt). She was frightened about having to go to live with her father. She explained that her father had a new wife, who had two children. They were all mean to her. She worried about something happening to her mother which would cause her to have to live with her dad. Everyone was supportive and talked about who they'd live with if something happened to their parents. In the beginning, Camille was very tense telling us about her fear, but she relaxed as the group gave her support and shared their fears about the same problem. Today was one of the first times Camille participated actively.

Kelly was afraid of doors. This related to an experience she told us about several months ago. A bomb had been left on the front porch and would have killed whomever opened the door. Fortunately, no one was home. She told about her fear of opening the front door, her bedroom door, and almost any door she couldn't see through. Kelly was able to recognize the pattern, and relate it later to Tim's

fear, which also had to do with a real life experience.

Tim was afraid that a man in New York would shoot him in the head with a machine gun. He was able to see that this related to his experience during the riots in Chicago when a man with a shotgun went berserk in a hospital where Tim and his friends sought refuge. Tim witnessed a policeman shoot this man through the head after he had killed a number of people. Everyone agreed that they would be afraid, too, and there was considerable discussion about being shot, stabbed, attacked, etc.

Arthur was afraid of cars driving up his driveway at night and stopping, and also strange noises at night. They live in a house with a long driveway on several acres of land. He explained that it's an old house and it makes lots of creaky, funny noises. He's afraid someone will come and try to rob them or hurt them if they know just the kids are at home with the housekeeper, who is Asian, limps badly, but is a "Black Belt in Samurai swords". There was a lot of joking about her abilities to protect them as well as keep them in line.

Bruce was afraid of going out alone to the barn at night to feed the animals. He explained that it's very, very dark and once you're out there, no one can see or hear you from the house if you need help. Arthur and Tim immediately empathized with Bruce, and they both related their experiences of being down at a store at night, about a block from their house and then walking back. They had decided they were too scared to stay down there. Every sound scared them more, until they were running as fast as they could to get home. Bruce decided to take his dog or another person with him in the future.

We had a valuable discussion today with everyone revealing a lot about their own fears as well as some mutual fears.

Lesson 43: Projected Fear

BEGINNING

Discuss examples of fears (from the homework assignment) that the children are comfortable sharing. Review the concept of projection.

AFFECTIVE EXPERIENCE

- The Mother and Father Projection Experiment

ASSIGNMENT

Write a journal entry about fears you used to have and about fears you still have.

COGNITIVE INQUIRY

1. "Do many people have fears about their personal safety? Do you? What kinds?"

2. "How can we use the Trumpet with these kinds of patterns?"

3. "Is it any easier to talk about fears?"

4. "Which of your fears seems to be similar to the fears of others?"

5. "What are some lessons from today? Where else could you use them?"

PROCEDURE

Going around the room one at a time, ask each student to describe her/himself as if her/his mother were talking. For example: "Johnny's a nice enough boy, but he acts kinda lazy. He never picks up his clothes...." Repeat this procedure as if the student were the father.

FOLLOW-UP

Discuss "I learned..." statements in a total group. Have the class make the appropriate journal entries.

DISCUSSION QUESTIONS

1. "I discovered that I..."

2. "If I had it to do over, I'd..."

The Mother and Father Projection Experiment

VARIATION

Do the projections in dyads or quads rather than going around the whole room one at a time. Have the students exaggerate their parents' behaviors.

This exercise is used to elicit and categorize students' concerns.

Lesson 44: Reflecting Concerns

BEGINNING

Review the steps in the Trumpet. Review: killer statements, confidentiality, projection, avoidance.

ASSIGNMENT

Write in your journal twenty words that express your positive feelings and ten words that express your negative feelings.

AFFECTIVE EXPERIENCE

- The Three Wishes Experiment.
- The "I wonder..." Statements Experiment.

MATERIALS

Newsprint, magic markers, Trumpet display

COGNITIVE INQUIRY

1. "Were there any patterns in the experiences?"

2. "Are you willing to share your 'I wonder...' statements'?"

3. "How similar are yours to others'?"

The Three Wishes Experiment

PROCEDURE

Ask the students, "If you suddenly were given three wishes, what would they be?" Give the students a few minutes to think about this and then ask for "wishes" to be shared with the class.

FOLLOW-UP

Students can discover similarities and differences in wishes by using the first two processing questions below. General areas of concerns can be noted on the board or newsprint. The class can then brainstorm ways to make wishes come true.

DISCUSSION QUESTIONS

1. "In what ways were your wishes like other students' wishes?"

2. "In what ways were yours unique?"

3. "Do you feel your wishes could ever come true?"

4. "How could you make them come true?"

This exercise can help students consider some of their concerns.

VARIATION

Have the group imagine a magic wand or a magical elf that can grant wishes.

The "I Wonder..." Statements Experiment

PROCEDURE

Ask students to make statements beginning with "I wonder . . ." (what, if, why, when, etc.). Examples: "I wonder why the teacher seems sad today," "I wonder if my parents will let me go out on the weekend."

To break through imitation patterns and to elicit deeper concerns, go around the class, one student after another, about three times. Watch for patterns of concerns emerging.

FOLLOW-UP

Ask students how they felt hearing others' statements. Ask if they noticed any similarities or differences in concerns.

DISCUSSION QUESTIONS

"Any new 'I wonder...' statements to make now that the exercise is over?"

"Any 'I learned . . .' statements?"

VARIATION

Ask students to pick a partner and take turns making "I wonder..." statements to each other.

This exercise is used primarily to elicit students' concerns. It can also be used at the end of any exercise as a process procedure.

NOTES FROM KAREN'S JOURNAL

We reviewed our projections from last week, beginning with people we liked. We also reviewed the concept that when we say things to other people, it may be something that's accurate about ourselves—positive or negative (i.e., re-owning).

We took a few minutes to review all the things the group remembered talking about during the year.

Boys and girls		
Explode	Dreams	Killer statements
Robots	Nonverbal	Imagination
Trustfalls and walks	Birthdays	Way you feel about yourself and
Camera	Good Times	other people
Consensus	Re-owning	Projections
Magic bag	Trumpet	Bad times
Likes	Hopes	Personal things
Break in	Fears	Learning about senses
Being absent	Rumor	Self-sciencing machine
Being confidential	Telephone	My birthday parties

LESSONS 45 — 49

Approaching Goal 9

Recognizing Present Behavioral Patterns; Learning About Learning Styles

Lessons 45 through 49 use all the tools developed in Self-Science to show students how to identify their own learning styles and those behavioral patterns with which they feel comfortable and which they are able to perceive.

GROUP BEHAVIOR

Learning about learning is an exciting pay-off. The group will be feeling a sense of pride and accomplishment, using and sharing their Self-Science tools for relatively independent inquiry. Help individuals in the group accept and apply their findings to their ongoing schoolwork. Individual conferences are appropriate here, if possible.

EVIDENCE OF AFFECTIVE GROWTH

• Demonstrating an increasing ability to identify and describe personal behavioral patterns.

• Identifying personal learning patterns.

• Demonstrating an increasing awareness of the consequences and functions of behavioral patterns.

EVIDENCE OF COGNITIVE GROWTH

• Learning about one's personal learning patterns.

• Integrating and using the cognitive tools taught to date.

Lesson 45: Thinking About Learning

BEGINNING

Discuss the idea that we learn in many ways. Why is it easier to learn some subjects than others? Do we learn differently on different days?

AFFECTIVE EXPERIENCE

- Together, review the self-inventory: "How Do I Learn?" Then brainstorm experiments or activities that could demonstrate these differences (e.g., role-play a learning situation; students could survey themselves for a week; invent a game; or pair up with a friend and then watch each other).

As you brainstorm, indicate the name of the person giving the suggestion. When the brainstorming is finished, suggest that there are personal styles in the kinds of suggestions people make. For example, the person suggesting role-playing may have a learning style that works best through physical activity, using the entire self to learn.

COGNITIVE INQUIRY

1. "Is one learning style better than another?"

2. "Can you learn in a style that is not your strongest? How?"

3. "What are some new lessons or tools you learned today? Where else could you use them?"

ASSIGNMENT

Write a short story about a student going to school and the challenges s/he faces in learning.

MATERIALS

Self-Inventory: "How Do I Learn?" (see page 118) one for each student.

NAME: _____

Self-Inventory: How Do I Learn?

Circle the numbers of the items you think are most like you. If you think more than one item is like you, circle more numbers.

A. I can learn best in the:

1. morning
2. middle of the day
3. afternoon
4. evening

B. I can learn something easily by:

1. reading it
2. hearing it
3. seeing it in pictures
4. writing it in my own words
5. explaining it to someone
6. drawing a diagram or picture of it
7. talking about it with somebody else
8. teaching somebody else

C. I dislike having to learn:

1. in big group meetings
2. in little group meetings
3. in game situations
4. with a partner who chose me
5. with a partner the teacher chose for me
6. with a partner I don't know
7. by myself
8. in team situations

D. While learning, the things that bother me the most are:

1. being in a quiet place
2. being in a noisy place
3. having a radio or television on
4. being interrupted
5. stopping before I'm through
6. having to wait for others to finish

E. I seem to do homework best with:

1. an hour or more to think
2. short work sessions
3. having a work routine

F. For learning by reading I like to:

1. ask questions before reading
2. skim before reading
3. ask questions after reading

G. My most difficult subject is:

The easiest for me is:

From Self-Science, McCown, Jensen et al. © 1998, Six Seconds.

The owner of this book has permission to copy this page for his or her classroom use.

BEGINNING

Review responses to A, B, C items on the "How Do I Learn?" questionnaire.

Lesson 46:
Learning Styles
Self-Inventory

AFFECTIVE EXPERIENCE

- In pairs, work on items D through G and complete answers on the Self-Inventory: "How Do I Learn?"

COGNITIVE INQUIRY

1. "Did you mark more than one possibility for item D? If you did, are they equally bad?"

2. "How did you mark item E? Do other people have the same responses? Is your pattern similar to the majority of others? Did you learn anything about this item from your Time-Diary study?"

3. "How did you mark items F and G? Have you ever thought about these questions before? When?"

4. "Do you sometimes get confused between whether you like a subject or a teacher? Can you like a teacher and not a subject? Vice-versa?"

5. "What other questions might be asked as items to put on the questionnaire? Put four of these items on the chalkboard and the possible alternatives. Brainstorm other questions that are important for how you learn."

6. "What do you do if you don't like a subject?"

ASSIGNMENT

Answer A, B, and C of the Self-Inventory: "How Do I Learn?" and write about the questions in your journal.

MATERIALS

Self-Inventory: "How Do I Learn?" (students to bring in).

Lesson 47: Multiple Intelligences

BEGINNING

Formal education is primarily directed towards linear, concrete, linguistic learners. As a part of learning about learning, it is important for students to understand this bias — particularly if they learn most readily in other modalities.

Introduce the term "metacognition" (thinking about thinking).

MATERIALS

Style Sort Cards, copy enough for each student or pair

AFFECTIVE EXPERIENCE

• The Style Sort Experiment

COGNITIVE INQUIRY

1. "What influences you to make the choices you did for A and B?"

2. "Why were your three sorts different?"

3. "Are there patterns you would like to change in the way you study and work?"

4. "What are some new lessons or tools you learned today? Where else could you use them?"

The Style Sort Experiment

PROCEDURE

Copy the Style Sort cards and cut them up, one set for each student (or pair). Individually or in pairs, have the students sort the Style Sort Cards and record the answers in their journals.

A. Sort from "most sucessful" to "least successful"

B. Sort from "I'd like to be..." to "I would not like to be..."

C. Sort from "most like me" to "least like me."

*This activity helps children see how their own points of view are like and unlike their peers. It shows a **literal** pattern, which can help explore the idea of internal patterns.*

DISCUSSION QUESTIONS

1. "How did you feel about sorting the cards?"

2. "Why are some 'successful'? Do you feel unsuccessful as a learner?"

Style Sort Cards

From Self-Science, McCown, Jensen et al. © 1998, Six Seconds.
The owner of this book has permission to duplicate this page for her or his own classroom.

Lesson 48: Group Behavior

BEGINNING

Provide an opportunity for students who didn't talk earlier to give information regarding their patterns, behavior alternatives, and possible choices.

MATERIALS

Continuum to Look at Group Behavior (one for each student)

AFFECTIVE EXPERIENCE

• Have the class complete the continuum exercises.

COGNITIVE INQUIRY

1. "What other type of continuum is applicable? Can you make up one?"

Continuum to Look at Group Behavior

PROCEDURE

Explain what a continuum is. Draw a continuum on the chalkboard.

"Withdrawn Wilma/Wilbur" <————————————> "Dominating Dave/Doris"

Direct the students to place themselves on the continuum in terms of the way in which they behaved in the group today.

Next, individually and silently on paper, have them place other members of their group on the continuum. Give the class time to permit individuals to check out their perceptions of personal behavior with the perceptions of others.

This exercise is useful for expanding the learner's capacity to look at personal behavior, to give and receive feedback, and to check perceptions of self with the way others perceive the learner. (Use names of both sexes so that sex role stereotypes will not be a variable.)

DISCUSSION QUESTIONS

1. "Did others place you at the same point on the continuum as you placed yourself?"
2. "Did you see yourself as other members of the group saw you?"
3. "Did you see others as they saw themselves?"
4. "Is the way you behaved today your usual way of behaving in the group?" (Use "I learned..." statements.)

FOLLOW-UP

In trios, share one another's "ranking" on the continuum; compare to your own.

VARIATIONS

Use other versions of a continuum. For example:

"Silent Sam/Sally" ——————————————— "Disruptive Roy/Ramona"

Lesson 49: Inner and Outer Perceptions

BEGINNING

Discuss the difference between the ways we see ourselves and the ways others see us. A subtle, but important, point is that other people's views of us are not always "right" — we should not change simply to suit others. If, however, Joe sees himself as funny and his friends see him as annoying, Joe may wish to re-evaluate the way he presents his humor.

Review ground rules.

AFFECTIVE EXPERIENCE

• Respectfully share the continuum assignments. Start in quad groups, then in larger groups.

COGNITIVE INQUIRY

1. "How closely did the perceptions of others match yours? How were the perceptions alike? How different?"

2. "Were you harder on yourself than the others?"

3. "How closely did your perceptions of others match their perceptions of themselves? How were they different?"

4. "What value is there in getting feedback about how others perceive you? Is it helpful? Does feedback help you consider your patterns?"

5. "Are there times when you shouldn't change your pattern? Who has the power to choose one behavior over another?"

6. "What are some new lessons or tools you learned today? Where else could you use them?"

ASSIGNMENT

Make a group-behavior continuum and put everyone on it where you **usually** see them. Possible topics are responsibility, sharing, listening.

NOTES FROM KAREN'S JOURNAL
Relating to Patterns and Discovering Patterns

One of the children confronted Robbie, fourth grade boy, with the fact that he always was disrupting the sessions, the discussions, and the activities by needing or having to be different. His usual pattern was either to sit on two or three bean bags or to sit on the piano or walk around the room or not to sit on the bean bags, etc. Robbie would engage in these activities in an obviously attention-getting manner.

After being confronted with this observation, Robbie owned that he did disrupt the group and that he felt the need to be different from everyone else. As we talked, it became apparent that his need to be different was related to his fear that he would not be accepted by the rest of the group if he went along with the members. Consequently, he adopted a rejection model. We asked him to explore alternatives and he was able to at least think of the idea of behaving as the other children did at the beginning of the session by coming in and sitting down and preparing to engage in the activities and discussions. He was able to try on this pattern, and as the year proceeded many of the children began to feel more positively toward him as a group member.

Approaching Goal 10

Experimenting With Alternative Behavioral Patterns

Lessons 50 through 52 focus on the process of changing behavior. Students choose a pattern they wish to change. They observe and conceptualize the change process.

GROUP BEHAVIOR

This may be the most difficult Goal for the group to understand and master. Some individuals may be unable to make this progress. Even so, becoming aware that changing one's patterns takes conscious awareness and effort can have value in accepting one's own limitations, tolerance for others, and development of realistic goals.

Trying on new behaviors or exploring alternative responses is a natural outgrowth of learning about patterns; it is usually the most difficult goal to attain. Surely it's unrealistic to expect all students to do this easily or often, without help. We all can see in our own behavior certain patterns (habits) which we seem to fully understand and yet are unable to change easily. Some of the most obvious patterns adults have in experimenting with alternatives include: smoking, irritation with a boss or secretary, having difficulty getting up in the morning, etc. People talk about alternatives to all these patterns, but actually experimenting with an alternative is the real challenge.

At first it is generally useful to focus on a group, or class pattern rather than on an individual pattern. Once alternatives have been explored, students can be asked to choose an alternative and try it.

If a Self-Science class has a pattern of boys sitting on one side, girls on the other, an alternative may be to sit boy/girl, boy/girl, etc. and then do some familiar activities such as Telephone Gossip or Trust Walk. Trying new patterns as a group feels less threatening.

Students need encouragement and support for trying on alternative behaviors. This support can be accomplished by overt praise from the teacher as well as by encouraging students to praise others and to express their feelings in relation to trying on alternative behaviors. Having the students express feelings about alternative behaviors is the beginning of the final and most important goal of evaluating behavior patterns.

EVIDENCE OF AFFECTIVE GROWTH

- Showing an increasing ability to conceptualize alternatives.
- Experimenting with new behaviors.
- Starting to accept personal limitations.

EVIDENCE OF COGNITIVE GROWTH

- Beginning to understand the process of making changes.

BEGINNING

Introduce and expand on the idea of alternative responses. (Read the introduction to this section.)

Review the parts of the Trumpet with special emphasis on alternative behaviors and choosing actions.

Lesson 50: New Risks

AFFECTIVE EXPERIENCE

• Complete the Secrets Improvisation Experiment.

COGNITIVE INQUIRY

1. "Could you identify the secrets with the person who wrote them?"

2. "Did you think others identified your secret?"

3. "Was your secret consistent with your usual pattern of behavior?"

4. "Could you think of alternative behaviors for the secrets offered?"

5. "Were the secrets given more risky than those offered earlier in the year? Why do you suppose this happened?"

ASSIGNMENT

Write two new secrets (not from Secrets in the Hat) in your journal; then write alternatives of how you can (could have) react(ed).

MATERIALS

blank paper (for each student)

PROCEDURE

Each person writes a secret about him/herself, no names included, on a blank piece of paper, folds it and drops it into a box. After the papers in the box are shuffled, each person draws a secret and keeps it folded until her/his turn comes.

The student then reads the secret aloud and **continues talking/improvising** as if the secret (and the hopes, fears, aspirations, and feelings) of the writer were his/her own. If by chance a student opens her/his own secret, that individual may either pass or read it as if it were someone else's.

The Secrets Improvisation Experiment

DISCUSSION QUESTIONS

1. "How did you feel when you heard your secret being read?"

2. "Did the reader react the same way you did?"

3. "How did you feel acting out someone else's secret?"

This exercise is used for practice in trying on a new behavior.

Lesson 51: Recognizing Alternatives

BEGINNING

Clarify the idea of patterns as habitual responses that have both positive and negative sides. Introduce the metaphor that the brain is a survival mechanism — if you were a lion, you would want your brain to follow patterns that kept you alive. But, since you are not a lion, you might want to make your own decisions.

ASSIGNMENT

In your journal, describe a conflict and identify your pattern.

AFFECTIVE EXPERIENCE

• Complete the Patterns to Sell Experiment.

COGNITIVE INQUIRY

1. "How did your commercial compare to the others? Which commercials might you accept?"

2. "How do you go about considering alternatives? Is it easy to think about other options?"

3. "How does one choose one behavior over another? What is used when new behaviors are tried? Can anything be gained? Can anything be lost? What does it take to try a new behavior?"

4. "Can anyone help you do this?"

5. "How do you decide whether the new behavior is better than the old?"

PROCEDURE

Students are asked to make a commercial for their pattern. Imagine your pattern as a medical potion. If someone were to take a dose of this potion, what would it do for them? Consequences of a pattern can be determined by listing dangerous side effects that must be written on the label of the potion.

Patterns to Sell Experiment

DISCUSSION QUESTIONS

Ask the students to think about the following questions when writing their commercials.

1. "What will this potion do for someone?"

2. "How much potion should be taken? How often?"

3. "What are its strongest selling points?"

4. "What would the warning label say?"

5. "What are some of the side effects of taking this potion?"

6. "How would the potion be packaged?"

7. "What would it sell for?"

8. "Is it cheap or expensive for someone to buy?"

This exercise is designed to highlight the "alternatives" and "choices" steps of the Trumpet.

FOLLOW-UP

Students can make posters or "storyboards" of their commercials. The class can give feedback as to how people felt about purchasing the pattern. Students can write in their journals about whether they would buy their own patterns — and about which other patterns they saw that they would or would not buy.

VARIATION

Students can design a commercial to present to the class in mock TV or radio presentations.

Lesson 52: Reasonable Choices

BEGINNING

Discuss idea of "choosing alternatives." Introduce the idea that sometimes it helps to talk with others about choices.

MATERIALS

Mars Lander "Individual Worksheet" and "NASA Response" on seperate sheets, (one for each student).

AFFECTIVE EXPERIENCE

• Complete the Mars Lander Experiment.

COGNITIVE INQUIRY

1. "Does it help to talk over possible choices with other people?"

2. "When might it help? When might it not help?"

3. "With whom does a final decision or choice always rest? Who has responsibility for action? When do you think the best decisions are made?"

4. "How can the Trumpet process help in thinking through decisions?"

5. "Are some people reluctant to talk over problems with others? Why aren't all problems talked over with others?"

The Mars Lander Experiment

This exercise is useful for expanding the learner's capacity to look at choices and to consider alternative actions. Further, the exercise is useful in helping the learner to at least consider talking over possible choices with others who may be helpful.

PROCEDURE

Pass out the Mars Lander Individual Worksheet, one page to each learner.

When they have completed the first part of the assignment, have them group into teams of five and answer as a group.

Next, hand out the NASA Response page and have each group compare their answers to NASA's.

DISCUSSION QUESTIONS

1. "Did you score as well when you made decisions by yourself as when you were working with other members of your team? How did you arrive at a decision for yourself? For members of the team?"

2. "Did it help to talk over possibilities with other people? How?"

3. "What did you do when as a team you couldn't agree on an answer?"

4. "Do all problems have a correct answer?"

5. "Was your behavior with the group similar to your usual behavior in groups?"

6. "What was helpful behavior on the part of others when group decisions were made?"

NAME: _____

Mars Lander: Individual Worksheet

The Situation

Your lander has just crash-landed on the lighted side of Mars. You were scheduled to rendezvous with a mother ship 200 miles away, but the rough landing has ruined your ship and destroyed all the equipment on board, except for the 15 items listed below.

Due to technical difficulties the mother ship cannot come to you. You must go to it. Your crew's survival depends on reaching the mother ship, so you must choose the most critical items available for the 200-mile trip. Your task is to rank the 15 items in terms of their importance for survival. Place number one by the most important item, number two by the second most important, and so on through number 15, the least important.

Box of matches

Food concentrate

Fifty feet of nylon rope

Parachute silk

Solar-powered portable heating unit

Two .45 caliber pistols

One case of dehydrated milk

Two 100-pound tanks of oxygen

Local star map

Self-inflating life raft

Magnetic compass

Five gallons of water

Signal flares

First aid kit containing injection needles

Solar-powered radio

Mars Lander

From Self-Science, McCown, Jensen et al. © 1998, Six Seconds.
The owner of this book has permission to copy this page for his or her own classroom use.

Mars Lander:
NASA Response

GROUP NAMES:

Supply	NASA's Rank	NASA's Reason	Your Rank
Box of matches	15	No oxygen on Mars to sustain flame; virtually worthless	
Food concentrate	4	Efficient means of supplying energy requirements	
Fifty feet of nylon rope	6	Useful in scaling cliffs, tying injured together	
Parachute silk	8	Protection from sun's rays	
Solar-powered portable heating unit	13	Not needed unless on dark side	
Two .45 caliber pistols	11	Possible means of self-propulsion	
One case of dehydrated milk	12	Bulkier duplication of food concentrate	
Two 100-pound tanks of oxygen	1	Most pressing survival need	
Local star map	3	Primary means of navigation	
Self-inflating life raft	9	CO2 bottle in military raft may be used for propulsion	
Magnetic compass	14	Earth compass won't work on Mars	
Five gallons of water	2	Replacement for tremendous liquid loss	
Signal flares	10	Distress signal when mother ship is sighted	
First aid kit containing injection needles	7	Needles for vitamins, medicines, etc., will fit special aperture in NASA space suits	
Solar-powered radio	5	For communication, only good for short range	

From Self-Science, McCown, Jensen et al. © *1998, Six Seconds.*
The owner of this book has permission to copy this page for his or her own classroom use.

Winding Up Goals 6-10

Lessons 53 — 54

Group Behavior

Now the group must make final preparation for terminating. You can aid this process by focusing on beginnings, middles, and endings, using the new tools. You may wish to schedule individual conferences for final evaluation.

Evidence Of Affective And Cognitive Growth

- Moving toward a satisfying sense of accomplishment and closure.

- Ability to apply Self-Science techniques independently.

Lessons 53 and 54 are the culminating lessons for the Self-Science program. As with the end of the course, a celebration or some sort of informal get-together is a good way to end.

The final lessons are OASIS, open to review and discuss the course and address any left-over issues.

> *The last lessons are intended to consolidate the work done during the program and leave the students with an awareness of the tools they now possess and some sense of when the tools are useful.*

Once a student has identified and examined current behavior patterns, explored the consequences and functions of these patterns, and experimented with alternative patterns, s/he needs to understand new behaviors in a similar manner. In this way, it's possible to enlarge the repertoire of available responses on any given situation.

The idea, in many instances, is not to abandon one pattern in favor of another, but rather to increase the available responses. For example, a child's pattern is to hit her younger brother when he sits between her and the television. The consequence is to be denied television by her mother. The function of her response is that short term, she feels better by "punishing" her brother. A reasonanble alternative behavior is to simply move — but while that avoids the consequence, **it does not serve the function**. So, she may decide to use her old pattern sometimes and the alternative at other times — but her awareness of alternatives is critical for her affective growth.

This last goal is primarily cognitive; in terms of Bloom's Taxonomy, this goal requires critical and evaluative thinking. Since this stage is about assigning value, it is important that the teacher refrain from imposing personal value judgments (i.e., one pattern is better than the other). The teacher should ask neutral guiding questions: "How did your alternative pattern serve you? When you think back on your old pattern and the new one, were there any differences in the way they made you feel? What were the differences? Are there times when you think your old pattern might serve you better than your new one? Are there any other alternative behavior patterns?"

When students are able to evaluate personal patterns of behavior and their alternative patterns of behavior, they are able to increase their own life direction. They have internalized the steps of the Trumpet process and are freer to choose how they will respond to others and to situations they encounter.

Lesson 53: Affirming Growth

BEGINNING

Wrap up important lessons, discuss the reason for self-evaluation.

Administer post-evaluation instrument (see Appendix D, page 155) and discuss similarities and differences between the earlier and later responses.

MATERIALS

Strips of paper, 3"x8" or index cards, 5 per student

AFFECTIVE EXPERIENCE

• Celebrations Give Away experiment

COGNITIVE INQUIRY

1. "Which was more fun, writing the attributes or giving them away? Why?"

2. "Have you changed as a group? How?"

3. "How do you know when you have changed as a group? As an individual?"

4. "What tests can you use to decide if the changes are positive?"

Celebrations Give Away

PROCEDURE

Hand out 5 strips of paper or cards to each student. Have each student write one positive attribute about him or herself on each (no "backhanded" compliments).

Put the students in groups of four to six, and have them put all their attributes face down in a pile in the middle; shuffle the pile.

Each student takes a turn picking up one attribute, reading aloud, then either giving it away or keeping it for him/herself. If the attribute is given, the recipient and the giver should look one another in the eye and the recipient should say "thank you." No other talking is allowed.

This activity is useful for self-disclosure, group building, and for students to celebrate one another's growth.

DISCUSSION QUESTIONS

1. "How did you feel when other people got 'your' attributes?"

2. "How did it feel to keep/give yourself attributes?"

3. "Why did some people end up with more attributes?" (You may wish to add a rule that everyone should end up with five attributes; there are benefits both ways.)

Adapted from Stephen K. Smuin.

BEGINNING

Some people have made great contributions to our world. Ask the children which people have made a difference (e.g., Edison, Fossey, Gandhi, Mother Teresa, Franklin D. Roosevelt, etc.) What attributes did/do those people exhibit?

Discuss the idea of setting goals — internal goals, like changing patterns, and external goals, like stopping pollution.

AFFECTIVE EXPERIENCE

- Adopt an Attribute Experiment.

COGNITIVE INQUIRY

1. "Which comes first, internal changes or external changes?"

2. "Who is responsible for each kind of change?"

3. "How do you decide if you meant to change or if you were pushed to change?"

4. "Does changing yourself change other people?"

5. Review all the Self-Science techniques, strategies and tools. Make a big web or chart and discuss when each one might come in handy over the summer vacation.

Lesson 54: Celebrate New Goals

ICE CREAM

PROCEDURE

Each student, dyad or small group identifies a person who is a model of making a positive difference in the world, and one of her/his key attributes that each student would like to emulate.

In dyads or teams, brainstorm a list of actions that demonstrate the attribute. Make a special "attribute journal" for the summer or holiday, and copy into it the attribute and actions.

Finally, make a "contract" to try out the actions — at least one a day. The contract can be between the teacher and each student, or between pairs or groups of students. It should include the actions each person will take, the expected results (internal and external), and a date on which the contractees will phone or write one-another to check in on progress. It also can include a plan for celebration.

Encourage your students (and yourself!) to check-off the actions every day that they perform them. They can also add more actions — or even new attributes — as needed.

The Adopt An Attribute Experiment

This is a goal-setting activity that focuses on daily actions that lead to significant change.

NOTES FROM KAREN'S JOURNAL

Today we had a party. While we were eating we asked how everyone was feeling about ending self-sciencing. One reply was:

"Sob, don't put me in a bad mood. Wish we could keep on. It's the last time so it seems important. We can do it next year with the same group. I really like it."

We asked, "What have we done in here? How would you describe self-sciencing?"

The students replied, "We can discuss things—brainstorm. Neat when we could talk and do experiments—truthful—confidential. Things we did were exciting. Worth it because we did lots of different things and talked about lots of things. In the beginning we did a lot of activities, and now we can really talk with each other."

We said, "Would you like to have self-sciencing in the summer?"

Everyone said, "Yes."

We kept bringing up the ending of the group as there was a lot of resistance and denial. We stressed that this group is unique and although we will be a part of many groups, this particular group with these particular people is ending. The group reminded us to share appreciations, so we went around the cirlce and gave one another compliments.

I asked, "what are some words to describe Self-Science?"

fun	no killer statements
body talk	make friends
explosion	families
truthful	interesting
interesting	learning
S.S. machine	fears
hearing/seeing	friends
appreciates	embarrassing
education	nonverbal
Trumpet	trusting
happy	scary
feelings	touching
senses	great communication
secrets	consensus
confidential	daydreaming

Section 4:
Appendices

Affective Education Index

DIRECTIONS

Consider each of the four statements to consider your level of support of Self-Science education. Answer each of the questions by circling the number on the continuum that most closely represents what you believe.

Not at all	If it wouldn't interfere with basic teaching/learning	Might agree if more were understood	Would agree in an ideal framework	Would agree and wish to do something about it
1	2	3	4	5

STATEMENT 1: **"Teaching/learning about one's self (thoughts, feelings, and behaviors) is legitimate in school."**

Do I believe:

a. that teaching/learning about one's self is legitimate in school? .... | 1 | 2 | 3 | 4 | 5 | 1a

b. students believe that teaching/learning about self is legitimate in school? | 1 | 2 | 3 | 4 | 5 | 1b

c. other teachers in the school believe that teaching/learning about self is legitimate in school? .... | 1 | 2 | 3 | 4 | 5 | 1c

d. the administration believes that teaching/learning about self is legitimate in school? .... | 1 | 2 | 3 | 4 | 5 | 1d

e. the student services & support personnel believe that teaching/learning about self is legitimate in school? .... | 1 | 2 | 3 | 4 | 5 | 1e

f. parents believe that teaching/learning about self is legitimate in school? | 1 | 2 | 3 | 4 | 5 | 1f

g. the Board of Education in the district believes that teaching/learning about self is legitimate in school? .... | 1 | 2 | 3 | 4 | 5 | 1g

STATEMENT 2: **"Learning words and concepts for negotiating emotions is important."**

Do I believe:

a. that learning words and concepts for negotiating one's emotions is important? .... | 1 | 2 | 3 | 4 | 5 | 2a

b. students believe that learning words and concepts for negotiating one's emotions is important? .... | 1 | 2 | 3 | 4 | 5 | 2b

c. other teachers in the school believe that learning words and concepts for negotiating one's emotions is important? .... | 1 | 2 | 3 | 4 | 5 | 2c

d. the administration in the school believes that learning words and concepts for negotiating one's emotions is important? .... | 1 | 2 | 3 | 4 | 5 | 2d

From Self-Science, McCown, Jensen et al. ©1998, Six Seconds. The owner of this book has permission to copy this page.

From Self-Science, McCown, Jensen et al. © 1998, Six Seconds. The owner of this book has permission to copy this page.

e.   the student services & support personnel believe that learning words and concepts for negotiating one's emotions is important? .... | 1 | 2 | 3 | 4 | 5 | 2e

f.   parents in the school believe that learning words and concepts for negotiating one's emotions is important? .... | 1 | 2 | 3 | 4 | 5 | 2f

g.   the Board of Education in the district believes that learning words and concepts for negotiating one's emotions is important? .... | 1 | 2 | 3 | 4 | 5 | 2g

STATEMENT 3: "Learning through experience is important."

Do I believe:

a.   that learning through experience is important? .... | 1 | 2 | 3 | 4 | 5 | 3a

b.   students believe that learning through experience is important? .... | 1 | 2 | 3 | 4 | 5 | 3b

c.   other teachers in the school believe that learning through experience is important? .... | 1 | 2 | 3 | 4 | 5 | 3c

d.   the administration of the school believes that learning through experience is important? .... | 1 | 2 | 3 | 4 | 5 | 3d

e.   the student services & support personnel believe that learning through experience is important? | 1 | 2 | 3 | 4 | 5 | 3e

f.   parents believe that learning through experience is important? .... | 1 | 2 | 3 | 4 | 5 | 3f

g.   the Board of Education in the district believes that learning through experience is important? .... | 1 | 2 | 3 | 4 | 5 | 3g

STATEMENT 4: "Affective awareness can contribute to cognitive growth."

Do I believe that:

a.   affective awareness can contribute to cognitive growth? .... | 1 | 2 | 3 | 4 | 5 | 4a

b.   students believe that affective awareness can contribute to cognitive growth? .... | 1 | 2 | 3 | 4 | 5 | 4b

c.   other teachers in the school believe that affective awareness can contribute to cognitive growth? .... | 1 | 2 | 3 | 4 | 5 | 4c

d.   the administration in the school believes that affective awareness can contribute to cognitive growth? .... | 1 | 2 | 3 | 4 | 5 | 4d

e.   the student services & support personnel believe that affective awareness can contribute to cognitive growth? .... | 1 | 2 | 3 | 4 | 5 | 4e

f.   parents in the school believe that affective awareness can contribute to cognitive growth? .... | 1 | 2 | 3 | 4 | 5 | 4f

g.   the Board of Education in the district believes that affective awareness can contribute to cognitive growth? .... | 1 | 2 | 3 | 4 | 5 | 4g

Transfer your responses from the previous pages.

Profile of Beliefs About Affective Education

	1	2	3	4	5	
ME						**SECTION A**
1a						
2a						
3a						
4a						
STUDENTS						**SECTION B**
1b						
2b						
3b						
4b						
TEACHERS						**SECTION C**
1c						
2c						
3c						
4c						
ADMINISTRATION						**SECTION D**
1d						
2d						
3d						
4d						
STUDENT SERVICES & SUPPORT PERSONNEL						**SECTION E**
1e						
2e						
3e						
4e						
PARENTS						**SECTION F**
1f						
2f						
3f						
4f						
BOARD						**SECTION G**
1g						
2g						
3g						
4g						

From Self-Science, McCown, Jensen et al. ©1998, Six Seconds. The owner of this book has permission to copy this page.

DISCUSSION

Transfer your answer to the Profile to compare your perspective with the larger learning community.

When the profile is completed, pause for a moment to consider how you felt as you were reading the statements.

Did you feel the questions surfaced any observations of value?

Did you feel silly?

Did you feel you were wasting your time?

Did you enjoy being a "Self-Scientist"?

There are, of course, no right answers to these questions. They are intended to demonstrate a key element of Self-Science education: observing the process of an experience is an important tool for affective and cognitive learning.

The Profile reflects your beliefs, at this moment, about yourself and elements of your educational community.

ANALYZING THE PROFILE

Section A averages above 3:

You seem to have an educational philosophy consistent with Self-Science. If you charted a 2 or 3 to any statement, you may want to do further thinking, reading, or discussion on that topic.

Sections B-G average 3 or below:

The environment for accepting Self-Science is less than totally positive. It will be challenging to implement a systematic program; perhaps you should start with a small, voluntary "trial program." You need to do additional groundwork to change perceptions about the importance of emotional intelligence. Consider additional groundwork to create a supportive climate before implementing a Self-Science program.

Sections C, D, E, F, G average above 3, but one part scores low.

Spend some time building consensus in the groups that scored above 3, and then in increasing awareness with the other groups. Clear, open dialogue about educational issues and outcomes will be essential.

Do I Have the Leadership Qualifications to Teach Self-Science?

Probably! This activity is designed to have you experience the conscious process of identifying your patterns, just as later you may help children find some of their own patterns.

Step 1: List the personal qualities or characteristics you believe a good teacher should have. List as many as you think are important, up to 9.

1.

2.

3.

4.

5.

6.

7.

8.

9.

Step 2: Compare your list with the discussion of leadership qualifications for Self-Science teachers from pages 21 and 27.

Step 3: Overall, are the lists in general agreement? How many qualities showed up on both lists? There is no expectation the lists should be the same, but comparing them should give you some perspective. Is there a fundamental conflict? Are there attributes you do not usually use as a teacher but really are a part of your personality?

If your list of attributes matches none of those listed on page 27, you may find Self-Science a frustrating program. It might be too process oriented for you, or perhaps the subject area just isn't compelling.

This script demonstrates a facilitator working through the Trumpet with a small group. Excerpts can also be used as a role-play activity.

The Cookie Monster Meets The Trumpet

TRUMPET PROCESS STEPS 1 AND 2

INTRO: "The room is ready for a party but no one has come in yet. Softly the door opens and a head peers inside. It is the Cookie Monster! He looks carefully around, sees that no one is there and tiptoes to the refreshment table. As fast as he can, he grabs all the cookies and gobbles them down. Just as he's finished, Mark, Jane, and two other kids come in. They are disappointed because there are no cookies left for them. The teacher goes over and talks to the Cookie Monster, Mark, and Jane about what just happened. S/he is going to have them try to remember what they did during this confrontation. A confrontation is just something that happens — something specific that happens. S/he is going to see what each of their reactions were to the situation. While talking with them, the teacher will try to have them describe some of their thoughts and feelings."

TEACHER: "First, Cookie Monster, you tell us a little about what happened. Tell us what you did from the time you came into the room until now." (recap)

CM.: "Well, I got to the party first and saw two plates of cookies. I love cookies so I ate all the cookies off both plates." (identification of situation)

TEACHER: "What were you thinking about as you looked around the room?"

CM.: "I was thinking about how hungry I was in my tummy. I saw the cookies and I wanted all of them. I started toward the table." (connection between thought and action)

TEACHER: "Okay, can you tell what kinds of things you were saying to yourself as you went to the table?" (internal sentences)

CM.: "I said, 'Oh, look at that plate. Look at all those cookies. I love cookies the best.'"

TEACHER: "You did not think of anything else at all?"

CM.: "No, just cookies. Just me and the cookies."

TEACHER: "What kind of feelings were you having?" (identification of feeling)

C.M.: "I was hungry."

TEACHER: "Where did you feel hungry? Can you show us?"

CM.: "Right here. My tummy was hurting a little be-cause I was so hungry."

TEACHER: "Was any other part of you hurting, or was your tummy the thing you felt the most?" (clarifying question)

CM.: "Just my tummy. I felt my tummy the most."

TEACHER: "What did you do?"

CM.: "Well, I went to the table and I looked over by the punch, and there were two plates of cookies and my tummy was real hungry and it was hurting a little. So I said, 'Make my tummy feel better,' and I took all the cookies and ate them."

TEACHER: "Did you think at all about the other kids? Did you have any second thoughts?"

CM.: "I don't think I thought about the other kids."

TEACHER: "No? Just the cookies?"

CM.: "Just the cookies."

TEACHER: "Did you think about getting caught?"

CM.: "No. I don't get caught. I eat so fast."

TEACHER: "How do you think the other kids, who came in later, felt?"

C.M.: "They know I like cookies the best. Maybe they didn't feel anything."

TEACHER: "How do you think they felt about what you did?"

CM.: "I don't know. I thought maybe they would be mad at me, but I wanted the cookies so badly I ate them anyway."

TEACHER: "Let's try and find out what some other people saw. Jane, you were the one that came into the room next?"

JANE: "The Cookie Monster is mean!"

TEACHER: "Oh? Tell me what just happened to you. What did you notice first?"

JANE: "No cookies."

TEACHER: "Is that the only thing you saw?"

JANE: "I was hungry too."

TEACHER: "And did you see anybody else in the room when you came in?"

JANE: "No, there was just this big monster."

TEACHER: "What was he doing?"

JANE: "Eating."

TEACHER: "And when you saw that, how did you feel?"

NOTE: Jane is not responding to the questions asked. We assume many students will have a hard time at first and the facilitator or teacher must keep refocusing him/her.

JANE: "A little scared because I wanted to eat the cookies, too.

TEACHER: "Just scared?"

JANE: "A little scared so I didn't go up to the cookies." (feeling causing behavior)

TEACHER: "Do you know what frightened you?"

JANE: "How big this monster is."

TEACHER: "Well, he might hurt you. Is that what frightened you?" (source of feeling)

JANE: "He might eat me."

TEACHER: "He might eat you?"

JANE: "Yes, he might eat me!"

TEACHER: "So then what did you do, Jane?"

JANE: "I stood in the corner and watched."

TEACHER: "Can you remember what you looked like when you were in the corner watching?" (clarifying question)

JANE: "Yes."

TEACHER: "What did you look like?"

JANE: "Scared."

TEACHER: "How do you look when you are scared?"

JANE: "Like I look now."

TEACHER: "Here's a mirror. Take a look at yourself." (confrontation)

JANE: "Oooh!"

TEACHER: "How does scared Jane look?"

JANE: "I see my shoulders are rounded over and cover my body a little. My face, I feel my lips twitching a little." (response)

TEACHER: "You're a little folded up?" (reflective listening)

JANE: "Yes."

TEACHER: "And so when you were in the corner, what kinds of things were you saying to yourself?" (internal sentences)

JANE: "When is that Cookie Monster going to finish eating?"

TEACHER: "So that what?"

JANE: "So I can get my cookies."

TEACHER: "So that was your big wish—that he would stop?" (reflective comment)

JANE: "Yes."

TEACHER: "How do you feel about the Cookie Monster now?"

JANE: "I think the Cookie Monster is very mean."

TEACHER: "And what would you do now? Would you try to be near him?"

JANE: "No."

TEACHER: "You want to stay away from him?"

JANE: "Yes."

TEACHER: "Mark, could you tell what happened to you?"

MARK: "I came into the room and he had done it again. There were no cookies."

TEACHER: "You saw him eating the cookies?" (reflective question)

MARK: "Yes. Well, I heard him burp, brush off his mouth, and there were no more cookies, as usual."

TEACHER: "So what did you do?"

MARK: "I shrugged my shoulders and I said, 'He did it again' and I looked around to see if maybe there was some other cookies that I could find in the corner somewhere. Maybe the bag was still there and they were going to bring out some more.

TEACHER: "You remember any of the kinds of feelings that you had at the time?"

MARK: "I felt a little angry."

TEACHER: "At whom?"

MARK: "At the Cookie Monster and I felt a little angry at myself."

TEACHER: "Really? What were you angry at yourself about?"

MARK: "He always is there ahead of me.

TEACHER: "Yes?"

MARK: "And I always say to myself, 'He's smarter and faster.'" (internal sentence)

TEACHER: "So how did you blame yourself?" (naming the feeling)

MARK: "I know he's going to do it because he always does it and I saw him walking in here, but I let him go into the room first. When I got here the cookies were gone. I should have known."

TEACHER: "So you are angry for not knowing what to do or what you should have done?" (reflective listening)

MARK: "Yes."

TEACHER: "So what did you do next? Where did you go?"

MARK: "I looked in the corners to see if there were any bags. There were no bags there, and there were no more cookies. I don't know, I just sort of said, 'Yeah, that's it. No cookies again. He got them.' So I walked away and went over to some of the other children who had just come in. It's still on my mind though. It really annoys me." (naming feelings)

TEACHER: "These are examples of unique and common responses, done by inventorying of things you said to yourself, the kinds of feelings you had, and the kinds of things you did in the situation. At our next session we'll go to the next part of the trumpet which is the step called 'identifying patterns of behavior.' A pattern is the way you usually behave in a situation. We'll talk to the Monster again and also to Mark and Jane."

STEPS 3 & 4

TEACHER: "Cookie Monster, when you come into a place is this something you usually do—immediately look for the cookies and eat them?"

CM.: "I think I always do—always look for the cookies first."

TEACHER: "Do you ever do anything different?"

C.M.: "Don't think so."

TEACHER: "No matter who is around, you grab them and eat them?"

C.M.: "No matter who's around. I get there first."

TEACHER: "That is your pattern, then." (identifying a pattern, Step 3 of Trumpet)

C.M.: "What's a pattern?"

TEACHER: "Your pattern is the thing you do most of the time."

CM.: "Yeah, I do that most of the time. My pattern is I get to the cookies first and eat all the cookies right away."

TEACHER: "No matter who else wants them?"

C.M.: "Every time. That's my pattern."

TEACHER: (to Jane) "Remember what you did? Is that something you are likely to do?"

JANE: "What do you mean—likely for me to do?"

TEACHER: "When you didn't get what you wanted, you got scared and then you went right into a corner."

JANE: "Well... yes."

TEACHER: "Do you usually do that?"

JANE: "Usually I just kind of move to the side."

TEACHER: "And then what?"

JANE: "I wait to see—yeah, I just wait."

TEACHER: "To see if things get any better?"

JANE: "Yes. I don't do anything."

TEACHER: "Is that your pattern?"

JANE: "Pattern?"

TEACHER: "The thing you do most of the time when something happens."

JANE: "Yes, yes, I do that."

TEACHER: "So could you tell me what your pattern is in a situation like that?"

JANE: "Yes. I think that if I can't get something I want, I just move away."

TEACHER: "And stay by yourself until things cool off a little?"

JANE: "Yes."

TEACHER: "Mark, you've heard the other two talk about their patterns. Did you think that you showed a pattern of your own?"

MARK: "I don't know."

TEACHER: "Is this usual for you? When you cannot get any cookies, you begin looking around for some more, and you also become angry at yourself for not knowing better?"

MARK: "Yes, I get angry at myself a lot of times when people get what I want, and I don't get any."

TEACHER: "Then you get angry at yourself?"

MARK: "Yes. Like I got angry because the Cookie Monster was quicker than me."

TEACHER: "You're a little bit angry at him, but you're also angry at yourself?"

MARK: "Yes, I get angry at myself."

TEACHER: "So when you are angry at yourself, what are you saying?"

MARK: "I'm saying I could have done better or I could have been smarter, or I could have been quicker."

TEACHER: "Is that something you say to yourself a lot?"

MARK: "Yes."

TEACHER: "That's your pattern. Could you say what your pattern is?"

MARK: "My pattern is that when somebody gets what I want or when I don't do what I would like to do, I blame myself and I say I could have been smarter, or I should have been faster or I'm not too good. That's my pattern."

TEACHER: "Each of you has identified a pattern. Now let's look at the way these patterns function for you— how they work for you. All right, Cookie Monster, can you tell me what your pattern is again?"

CM.: "My pattern is when I come into a new place, I look for the cookies right away and then eat them up very fast."

TEACHER: "How does that work for you?"

CM.: "Oh, it makes me feel very good because it fills up my tummy and makes me smile because the cookies taste so good. Makes me feel very good to be first and get all the cookies." (identifying how a pattern functions—Step 3 of the Trumpet)

TEACHER: "So that pattern really helps you?"

CM.: "Oh, yeah. Because then I get all the cookies."

TEACHER: "Right. And what happens to your stomach when you eat all the cookies?"

CM.: "Oh, my stomach feels good. It's all filled up."

TEACHER: "So the hurt moves away a little bit?"

CM.: "Oh yeah, the hurt moves away then."

TEACHER: "So that pattern really helps you? It lets the hurt go away and gives you a nice sweet taste in your mouth."

C.M.: "Oh, yeah, it tastes so good."

TEACHER: "And even when you're not eating cookies, you can think about how good it was when you ate them."

C.M.: "I think about it for a long time afterwards. I think about cookies a lot."

TEACHER: "Jane, can you tell me what your pattern is again?"

JANE: "When I can't get what I want, I feel sad and I just leave."

TEACHER: "Tell me, when you leave, how does that help you—to kind of pull away and go to a quiet place for awhile?"

JANE: "I don't know."

TEACHER: "You don't know how it helps you? How would that be compared to something else? Like suppose you had jumped up to the Cookie Monster and said ..."

JANE: "No! No! I would be too afraid."

TEACHER: "So going away helps you be less afraid?"

JANE: "Yes. I'm not so afraid when I'm far away."

TEACHER: "You are much less scared and don't have to get into things that are too scary?"

JANE: "I just wait until things get better."

TEACHER: "Mark, remember what your pattern was?"

MARK: "Yes, I blamed myself. I should be smarter, or faster, or better."

TEACHER: "All right. It is blaming yourself for not being good enough. What do you think is good about that?"

MARK: "Well, sometimes I get smarter the next time. I say, 'I'm not going to let that happen again to me. I'm going to be better next time,' and then sometimes I really am. And I think one of these days I'm going to get the cookies first."

TEACHER: "Right. So, if you keep correcting yourself and seeing where you are weak, you might know better the next time and you will be stronger."

MARK: "That's right!"

STEP 5

TEACHER: "All right, Cookie Monster, we are back to you again. Let's see now, we are coming to the consequences part of the trumpet."

C.M.: "What's consequences?"

TEACHER: "When you buy something, you pay for it. Did you ever buy cookies, by the way?"

CM.: "No, I never bought any cookies."

TEACHER: "Remember you told me about what good happens—you feel so much better when you get all those cookies to eat and the pain in your stomach goes away and everything. Does anything bad happen when you do that?"

CM.: "Sometimes I don't have many friends."

TEACHER: "That's a consequence. Sometimes that is what happens. There are two things that happened to you. You get to feel good. Your pain goes away. You get those nice sweet tastes in your mouth. That one is a function, a good thing that happens to you. But another thing that happens, too, is that sometimes you don't have as many friends as you would like to have, or your friends get angry and won't talk to you and that makes you feel bad. That is a consequence."

CM.: "Oh."

TEACHER: "Jane, when you go away, one of the things that happens to you is that you feel less afraid. That is the way going away helps you. Is there anything about what you do that is not helpful?"

JANE: "I don't get my cookies."

TEACHER: "You don't get your cookies. So sometimes by going away you give up getting the things you want."

JANE: "No, sometimes people feel so sorry for me that they bring me cookies."

TEACHER: "That is the good part about their feeling sorry for you."

JANE: "Yes."

TEACHER: "Is there anything that makes you feel bad about their feeling sorry for you?"

JANE: "Yes, sometimes."

TEACHER: "What might bother you about that?"

JANE: "They might say 'Look at her. She can't do anything for herself.' I don't like that. I want to do things for myself."

TEACHER: "So it makes you feel a little smaller?"

JANE: "Yes, I feel small already."

TEACHER: "So some of the good things that help are: sometimes you feel much less frightened and sometimes people feel sorry for you and you do get the things you want. But a lot of times you don't get what you want, and when people feel sorry for you, you feel smaller."

JANE: "Yes."

TEACHER: "Mark, let's talk about the consequences of your pattern. You said before that when you tell yourself that you're not as good as you could be, it helps you do better the next time."

MARK: "That's right. Next time I'm going to get those cookies."

TEACHER: "So that's a function. Is there any kind of consequence that's not so good when you say that to yourself? Is there anything bad about saying that?"

MARK: "I don't know. I know I'm going to get the cookies. I'm going to get the cookies eventually I say that to myself, 'The next time, I'll be better.' So I'm not sure there's anything bad."

TEACHER: "You're not sure there is anything bad at all?" (clarifying question)

MARK: "No. Well, I get a little nervous."

TEACHER: "What do you mean, nervous?"

MARK: "Like I'm not going to be able to get them better than the Cookie Monster... and I feel bad that he's better than me. I'd like to be better than him."

TEACHER: "So, it would really be nice if you were as good as he is. Then you would be able to get what you want. That would be really nice." (focusing on the positive)

MARK: "Yes."

STEP 6

TEACHER: "Cookie Monster?"

CM.:   "Yeah?"

TEACHER: "Let's try to imagine a situation or a thing happening in which the results would be mostly good, rather than some good and some bad. I wonder if there is a way you could have cookies and still have friends? Would you think about that a little bit? And maybe we could all help you imagine ways. We will make up ways in which you could have cookies and have friends."

CM.:   "I have an idea. Do you think somebody could

teach me to bake cookies myself? And then I could give one to Jane and I could give one to Mark. And then they could be my friends and I could eat all the rest."

TEACHER: "Good! Then let us see how many different ideas we might have. Like one idea I have is maybe you could learn to like some other things, too, like apples, bananas, candy bars, and ice cream."

CM.:   "I never tried those."

TEACHER: "Spinach?"

CM.:   "I don't know. I never tried it. Is it good, too?"

TEACHER: "Well, right now you only have one thing to pick, right? Cookies. They're the only thing."

CM.:   "But I love cookies."

TEACHER: "I know, but they are the only thing that makes you feel good. Do you know if there is anything else that can make you feel good, too?"

CM.:   "I don't know."

TEACHER: "Well, maybe you would want to try it and see if there is anything else that could give you the same good feelings as cookies do, because if you could find more than one thing that makes you feel good, you would not have to go after only one thing."

CM.:   "Maybe I could try something new."

MARK: "Cookie Monster, I have a lot of candy. Candy is very good and maybe you'd like to trade candy for cookies."

CM.:   "I don't know. Maybe I could try it. I never ate candy."

MARK: "It's very good."

CM.:   "Very good? Does it taste like cookies?"

MARK: "Yeah, very much like cookies. But it tastes different too."

CM.:   "It tastes different? Maybe I could try one."

MARK: "You give me cookies and I'll give you candy."

CM.:   "Maybe I could try that."

MARK: "I'll give you ice cream."

CM.:   "What's ice cream?"

MARK: "You don't know what ice cream is?"

CM.:   "I never tried it. I only eat cookies."

MARK: "Oh, it's so great. Ice cream and cookies are good together. Ice cream is cold and it's sort of sweet like cookies and it's sometimes crunchy like cookies."

CM.:   "Crunchy? I like crunchy."

TEACHER: "What you just talked about are different ways of experimenting with *try-ons*. So you, Cookie

	Monster, may try candy and may try ice cream. Just to see. It may be that you don't like anything as well as you like cookies. But how will you know if you never try anything else? All right, Jane, let's think about what the best results for you would be. What kind of situation could get you what you want and help you to be less scared? Does that sound like it would be the best idea?"
JANE:	"You mean to be less scared and get what I want? Oh, yes."
TEACHER:	"It would be the best idea?"
JANE:	"Oh, yes."
TEACHER:	"Do you have any ideas that you could experiment with to get what you want and yet be less scared? Or, can anybody else think of any ways?"
JANE:	"Need courage."
TEACHER:	"Like the lion in the 'Wizard of Oz'?"
JANE:	"Yeah."
MARK:	"You could try what I do. You could try to get there first next time, and get the cookies first."
TEACHER:	"Or you could say to yourself that you're just not going to be afraid of that Cookie Monster."
JANE:	"Oh, no, no, no! He's too big. But I could get a friend who's bigger."
TEACHER:	"Hey, that is another one. Say that again. What could you do?"
JANE:	"Make friends with somebody else who's just as big as the Cookie Monster."
TEACHER:	"And what? He could protect you?"
JANE:	"Yes."
CM.:	"Jane, if you'd be my friend, I'd give you one of my cookies."
JANE:	"Well, that's OK, too, Cookie Monster."
CM.:	"And maybe I could even protect you."
TEACHER:	"You're looking at the Cookie Monster now. You said earlier you were too afraid to look at the Cookie Monster."
JANE:	"I feel a little different now."
TEACHER:	"You do?"
JANE:	"Yes."
TEACHER:	"What is helping you do that?"
JANE:	"Well, the Cookie Monster asked me to be his friend and he seemed to like that."
TEACHER:	"And that made you feel better?"
C.M.:	"It made me feel good."
TEACHER:	"So one experiment that you could try is talking to the thing you're afraid of."

JANE:	"Yes, that helped. Wow!"
CM.:	"Okay that makes me feel good."
JANE:	"Good."
MARK:	"You could come with me next time. We could both try to get there first together."
JANE:	"All right."
CM.:	"But you better save me a cookie if you get there before me."
MARK:	"Oh, I'll share them. We won't eat them all. We just want a couple."
CM.:	"Thank you, Mark."
TEACHER:	"Mark, what could you do to try on some new behavior?"
MARK:	"I could try saying to myself, 'you're not dumb just because you didn't get the cookies.' Also, maybe I could say, 'It wasn't all my fault that I didn't get the cookies.' Also, 'Well, it's not only me. Maybe I could be with somebody else next time. It's not only up to me.'" (examining alternatives)
TEACHER:	"Do any of you have any other ideas or experiments Mark could try?"
JANE:	"You could say to yourself, 'Cookies aren't that important. Why should I worry about them?'"
MARK:	"Yeah, I like other things."
TEACHER:	"But you like cookies a lot."
MARK:	"Yeah, I like cookies a lot. Yeah, I do."
JANE:	"Why couldn't you just talk to the Cookie Monster?"
TEACHER:	"Like Jane did?"
MARK:	"Yes."
JANE:	"And maybe the Cookie Monster will share more with you."
MARK:	"You know, I just never thought of talking to the Cookie Monster. I wasn't afraid of him. Maybe a little—a little afraid because I think he's better than me, faster and smarter."
CM.:	"I'm very fast."
JANE:	"But the Cookie Monster is clumsy and you're not clumsy"
MARK:	"Yes, that's true. I might talk to the Cookie Monster."

STEPS 7 AND 8

NARRATOR:	"A week later the teacher visits the class again. The purpose now is to evaluate the experiments."
TEACHER:	"Hey Cookie Monster, did you try any experiments this week?"

CM.: "Yeah, remember my pattern about getting all the cookies first?"

TEACHER: "Yes."

CM.: "Well, I saw Jane, and Jane gave me some candy and I gave her a lot of my cookies back. And I tried the candy and it was chocolate, like chocolate chip cookies, and it was crunchy. It was real good! I liked it. So now Jane and I are friends and now I like some kinds of candy. Now I have two things I like. I like cookies—still like cookies very much—very much. But now candy... candy is very interesting."

TEACHER: "In addition, you have a friend, too."

CM "Oh, that's real good. And Jane's not so quiet, and I can talk to her. She's my friend, kind of."

TEACHER: "So what would you say about your experiment? Do you like what happened?"

CM.: "Oh yeah. I feel really good now. Now I've got two things to eat. I've still got my cookies. Jane's my friend now. I've got somebody to talk to and she's not afraid of me."

TEACHER: "Thank you, Cookie Monster. Jane, did you try an experiment this week with your pattern?"

JANE: "Well, I kept talking to the Cookie Monster."

TEACHER: "And how did that make you feel?"

JANE: "I was scared. The Cookie Monster didn't know it though. So that made it easier."

TEACHER: "Did you feel less scared when it was easier?"

JANE: "Yes, I got less scared and it made it easier."

TEACHER: "What did you do that was different?"

JANE: "I went up to the Cookie Monster — 'approached' him."

TEACHER: "You used to go away."

JANE: "Right. I used to hide. But I went right to the Cookie Monster."

TEACHER: "Right to the thing that you were afraid of?"

JANE: "That's right. It was different. I didn't hide."

TEACHER: "And do as many people feel sorry for you?"

JANE: "No."

TEACHER: "Do you have any feelings about that?"

JANE: "Yeah, I feel good."

TEACHER: "Do you think you might try that again sometime—to talk to the thing that you are afraid of?"

JANE: "I don't know. Yes, I guess so.

TEACHER: "Mark, what happened with your experiment?"

MARK: "Well, I said to myself, 'You're not dumb just

cause you couldn't get the cookies.' 'Cause it happened again the next day."

TEACHER: "It did?"

MARK: "Yeah. The Cookie Monster the next day got there ahead of me, with Jane, and they got the cookies and candy, too."

TEACHER: "My goodness!"

MARK: "And I said to myself, 'You're not dumb. You're not dumb because this happened.'"

TEACHER: "Can I suggest a feeling, and you tell me if it fits?"

MARK: "Sure."

TEACHER: "Was the feelng like, 'I don't feel good about not getting the cookies. I'm disappointed, but not dumb. But I wish I had gotten them. That's the way the cookie crumbles.'"

MARK: "Well... I know I'm not dumb. I still want the cookies, though."

TEACHER: "So you only felt half as bad as you used to feel before, because you used to feel inferior for not getting the things you wanted."

MARK: "I still felt a little dumb. I said that to myself, that I still felt a little dumb. But I didn't feel as bad as I did before. And I also didn't think as much that I have to get there first."

TEACHER: "And what does that do for you? When you don't feel that you have to get there first?"

MARK: "I don't feel so nervous inside."

TEACHER: "You're more relaxed?"

MARK: "Yes."

TEACHER: "You like the feeling of being more relaxed?" (reflective listening)

MARK: "Yes, I felt better. I wasn't even nervous that night when I went to sleep. I wasn't thinking about how I didn't get the cookies or how dumb I was and how the next day I had to get there first."

TEACHER: "The most important thing now in completing the Trumpet experience is time. You need time to continue your experiments and see if this is a behavior you want to use more often."

CM.: "Then what?"

TEACHER: "Then you make a choice. If you do like this new way of behaving, then you may want to keep it as another way of acting. If you decide you don't like it, then there's no reason to keep it. The best thing about the Trumpet is that you can make your own choice after trying on something new."

Appendix B: Acceptance for Self-Science In Your School Or Program

The approach one takes in initiating a Self-Science curriculum naturally depends upon the particular structure and expectations of the school / district / program. Needless to say, introducing a totally new paradigm is a challenge. You must assess the potential level of acceptance by the superintendent, principal, fellow teachers, other staff, parents, and students. Depending upon the particular situation, it is reasonable to do some informal surveying of colleagues before making any formal presentation.

There are two kinds of support to be looked for in terms of informal surveying of colleagues; both are important and necessary for the success of the program and your sense of well-being. The first support to be assessed relates to colleagues' general awareness and feeling of importance for affective development. Find out both who thinks affective education is important and who thinks it is not important and who thinks it should not be taught in school. There are shades of gray between these poles. It is important to know, generally, who will support an affective program and who will oppose it.

The second support to be assessed relates to who else on the staff is willing to try such an endeavor. This support is very important, as it will likely influence the success of the Self-Science classes with the students and parents. Be sure to talk with the school psychologist; s/he often possesses valuable skills, as well as status, and can be very helpful in insuring a fair test of the curriculum. And, of course, enlist the support of the administration.

Assuming that you receive sufficient support to proceed, plan to make a formal presentation about Self-Science. There are several alternatives for doing this.

One alternative is to bring in an outside expert in Self-Science to do the presentation. This helps validate the program: it provides your staff with the resource of a recognized authority in the field, and it generates interest from the larger school community. This can be approached a number of ways, from an informal meeting with a small team to a whole-school inservice day. Some schools have sent a series of small groups of teachers to Six Seconds' workshops on emotional intelligence so they build enthusiasm in the community over time.

If you can't manage this, give a joint presentation with other interested teachers. Visit the Six Seconds' web site for current research and presentation materials at www.6seconds.org. Structure your presentation around the concepts from Section 1, particularly pages 1-4.

Remember to:

1. Adopt an open, candid attitude toward colleagues in the school. A comprehensive program requires faculty to treat one another the way students should treat one another.

2. Solicit feedback; jointly identify criticism, concerns and other obstacles. Together, brainstorm possible solutions — it isn't necessary to decide on solutions, simply to recognize that there are options if problems arise.

2. Build awareness that Self-Science is a comprehensive approach. It is complex, long-term, and relatively time-consuming. On the other hand, it works. In fact, research shows that programs that take this comprehensive approach are the ones that make a long-term difference. See "Effective Affective Programs, page 28.

3. Invite ongoing feedback and participation from the school community. A major objective of the course is to promote dialogue about feelings — so the more the staff talks about how kids are feeling, the better! Self-Science is a flexible, adaptable program, and input is necessary.

4. Team with other disciplines on Self-Science homework.

5. Explain the difference between "maintaining confidentiality" and "secrecy" (see Trust and Privacy, page 25). It is critical that concerns from Self-Science cross-over to the school and vice-versa.

Introducing
Self-Science To Parents

When you have gained the support of your school's administration and faculty, inform parents about this new subject, Self-Science. Again, it is valuable to bring in an expert to back-up your program.

In most school settings, the introduction of a new subject matter to the curriculum is always greeted by parents with a variety of responses: those totally opposed; those mildly curious or apprehensive; those strongly supportive and enthusiastic.

Knowing this, you will want to determine how to communicate about Self-Science as clearly and persuasively as you can. For key points, refer to pages 1-4 and to Six Seconds' web site (www.6seconds.org). Parents should know that Self-Science:

— supports the development of emotional intelligence skills that will help students solve problems, take responsibility for learning, and build stronger relationships. Review the major areas of emotional intelligence, including self-knowledge, self-control, motivation, empathy, social skills, and commitment to noble goals;

— is concerned with preparing students to manage the situations that concern them now. It does not teach them a new set of values or morals, but rather tools and skills to communicate and make thoughtful decisions;

— uses the methods of scientific inquiry to teach students to see themselves both as individuals and as part of a group, including opportunities to learn about their own learning styles and study habits;

— supports students in the developmentally normal issues and struggles of growing up — it is neither psychology nor therapy;

— is derived from decades of educational theory, learning theory, and child development, as well as from 30 years of testing and application within school situations.

— if you are offering Self-Science as an elective, let them know it is optional.

These ideas are best communicated face-to-face; an evening meeting with twenty to twenty-five people attending is ideal. Separate meetings for different grade or levels is advisable. A group which is too large makes it difficult to have good discussions.

If a small meeting isn't practical, consider scheduling a series of meetings, or making a brief introduction at a large meeting, such as a Back to School evening early in the semester; invite interested parents to a subsequent workshop. Also, make sure parents know that you welcome their questions and their feedback.

Meetings for parents can be presented in a variety of formats. It is valuable for parents to experience one of the Self-Science Experiments and follow-up discussion so they know the process first hand.

Most importantly, they should feel comfortable and leave the meeting with new knowledge and excitement about Self-Science. Most parents welcome techniques which make their parenting more productive, so provide specific skills.

Finally, your approach to Self-Science should let parents know you are on their side. Reassure them that Self-Science is not threatening to them personally, nor to their value systems, nor lifestyles. It does not teach a particular set of values: it helps students apply the values that their family has taught.

Four common questions and answers listed on the next page.

Four Common Questions and Answers

1. Q: Is Self-Science really important to the education of my child?

A: Yes. In the teaching-learning process, there are not enough chances to focus on the learner and the learning processes. By setting aside a small amount of time each week to help students study themselves, there will be short-term and long-term benefits. Children who take Self-Science will show more active participation in school life, a greater sense of responsibility, and greater self-confidence. Research shows that 70-80% of success is determined by the strength of an individual's emotional intelligence.

2. Q: What happens if my child reveals personal family matters?

A: The real focus on Self-Science is "self," and we focus our efforts toward understanding ourselves and our own behaviors. Sometimes family issues arise, but one of our ground rules is to not talk about people who are not present. In those cases, what is most likely is that your child will come home with some strategies to discuss with you. Self-Science does deal with relationships, though, and some activities ask children to think about their relationships at home. Again, the result is that children go home and talk to their parents.

3. Q: Can parents observe? Why is confidentiality a part of the class?

A: Confidentiality is important to the children. Few children are willing to reveal that they are afraid of the dark, have a nickname they hate, the fact that they still have stuffed animals they love, or a problem with a friend, unless they know all other members of the group will keep this information confidential. Few children are willing to try new ways when someone unfamiliar is watching.

Crucial to the group are the feelings of mutual respect, acceptance, and trust. Without these feelings, there is little, if any, chance students will feel comfortable enough to participate fully. Once the group has established those feelings, they may choose to allow a few visitors. It has to be up to the students to support their senses of confidence and power, so if you want to visit, ask your child to bring the question to her peers.

There is certainly no objection to your children telling you all about the experiences and activities they have in Self-Science class and their own responses. We only request that they keep others' responses confidential. Children enjoy knowing they are trustworthy and able to trust others.

4. Q: What happens if a child reveals deep personal problems?

A: Self-Science is not designed as therapy and is not intended to deal with individual, serious emotional issues. The focus of Self-Science is to teach cognitive processes for recognizing and coping with internal states, and not the revelation of unconscious conflicts.

Just like any class, though, teachers are required to report any suspicions of abuse or endangerment. Likewise, if a serious emotional need were to appear, the teachers would attempt to work with the child individually in the immediate situation, as well as consult with the principal, school psychologist (if any), and parents, following essentially the same procedures if the concern were noted during language arts, math, or recess time.

Appendix C: Group Development and Process

Self-Science involves a group; it is a people-centered curriculum. Much of the content comes from the members of the group and, in order to attain the curriculum goals, the collective individuals must progress through various states of group growth. Progressing through these stages — with constant awareness and discussion — is part of the Self-Science learning.

The stages are indicated as much as possible in the lesson plans, but your general awareness that a group develops and grows helps you in terms of your own expectations and demands. Formal groups usually have beginnings, middles, and endings.

BEGINNING

The beginning stage of the group is a slow, maturing process. Members are usually anxious. They question; they do not immediately feel a group solidarity; they are discovering the purposes for their meetings.

Students test limits with teachers and peers, building a feeling of security in their relationships with one another. During this time, students begin gravitating toward particular students, forming alliances or subgroups.

This is a critical stage of growth; children need to feel the support of at least one other student to begin to achieve a deeper level of honesty. Alliances should be allowed to develop. Alliances, however, can become detrimental to the group's work if they are allowed to become exclusive over long periods of time.

Encourage members of the alliances to relate to other members of the group, once security has been found. Ask students to choose different partners in various games and activities.

Frequently, the strongest alliances develop among children of the same gender. Bridging these alliances is often difficult; midway through the program, attempt to increase the size of the alliance and help those students be more inclusive. (This is also developmental; for example, fourth graders are often so uncomfortable with mixed

gender pairs that they do not engage in the Experiment. You might choose to mix them to teach a different, valuable, lesson about getting along with the other gender, but you need to be clear on your objective.)

Children you identify as leaders can be extremely helpful. These children are usually the most likely to cooperate; they are probably the most secure within their peer group. Shy or retiring students are more likely to cooperate once peer leaders have agreed to participate.

Group cohesiveness, a group life, and group work will emerge when students are relatively secure.

Part of establishing cohesiveness is establishing trust. Trust is dealt with quite consciously in the Lessons 5 to 10 of Goal Two, where specific ground rules for confidentiality are discussed quite thoroughly. Seeking trust, however, is a never-ending effort. You will be dealing with the building of trust from start to finish. After all, the deeper levels of trust permit deeper and deeper personal exploration, the essence of Self-Science.

MIDDLE

The middle stage of the group process proceeds, roughly, through two levels: At first, students will explore similarities and differences among themselves, focusing on similarities. Students find out if other members of their group have similar family backgrounds and experiences, similar fears, similar hopes, similar tastes in food. Emphasize similarities at this point because "similarity" sharing is safer emotionally.

You can strengthen your group at this point by focusing on positive attitudes expressed by one student for another. Encourage students to work in a supportive constructive manner rather than a destructive manner. Again, the lessons and activities will help you accomplish this.

Next, after they feel relatively safe in the group, students are often ready to move to the next level, which involves greater self-exploration. Focus is on the differences among group members and the personal meanings of these differences. Here, you assure and reassure the group that we are all positively and uniquely different from others in at least some ways. You will point out the "similarity of our differences."

During this middle-stage, your sensitivity to the students' needs for belonging helps keep the group in balance. Guide discussion and activities so that each member reveals a similar degree of information about self. This procedure avoids the possibility of one student feeling s/he revealed too much, or another student feeling inadequate because s/he couldn't reveal as much.

Somewhere during all this, there is a point when members need to rebel and test, either you or others. (This testing is called "storming" in the group development process of "forming, norming, storming, performing.") Be listening for expressions of hostility and expect that with some openness and support from you, it will pass. Hostility provides a safety valve. In some ways, it's your clue that the process is working. Indifferent people don't usually waste time testing. A "storm before the calm" can be read as a need to feel accepted in all ways, and thus safe.

In this testing process (which can occur many times during the development of a group), keep your long-term goals in mind. Recognize that testing is normal and make sure the child feels accepted — even though you might not accept the behavior. Do not allow a few disruptive individuals to sidetrack the group. Recognize that the feelings generated are real without escalating or counter-attacking on your part. You may want to try to discover the causes of the rebellion and confront them consciously at a later time. You may decide to ride it out. If your communication with the group seems relatively open (and only you can be the judge of that), you may want to propose that the group become aware of and deal with the hostility.

As all these diverse explorations take place, the major work of self-knowledge is occurring. Students are acquiring the tools for examining themselves, their feelings, their

patterns of response to others, their study and learning styles. The effectively functioning group, the performing group, is greater than the sum of its parts.

ENDING

The final stage of the group is, naturally, closure. Children as well as adults usually have difficulty dealing with endings. Children in Self-Science classes resist talking about the end of the class. Although you shouldn't force it, you would be wise to begin mentioning ending at least one month before the last meeting. Discuss endings in other situations and how they are like beginnings in some ways, to help the group deal with the termination of their class and recognize their own response to the ending. Provide an experience to provide closure. Repeat a favorite activity, go to a favorite spot, or have a quiet talk where everyone tells their favorite thing about the group.

Be aware, not every group proceeds to the same level or at the same rate. Nor is the progression even. Expect to spend at least half of a year's class establishing the climate and trust described.

DISCIPLINE

In a more traditional setting, "discipline" would also be an issue of this process; indeed, group dynamics can include discipline, but the goal here is a style of classroom management that demonstrates the spirit of Self-Science. "Discipline" is usually a process of the teacher wielding power, and while the Self-Science teacher still has more power than the students, to create the appropriate climate, you might leave that aside and focus on executing the ideals of respect and trust in very specific ways.

First, you can model that more-equal power through shared decision-making. Solicit input from the class, discuss options, and where appropriate, let them decide. Shared decision-making is not democracy — it simply means that the decision maker accepts input from interested parties.

Another way to help children feel important is to share problems with them (shared problem solving). The daily logistics and squabbles and interruptions can be ping-ponged back to the group for solutions. At first, their solutions might not work, but as with shared-decision making, they will learn from modeling.

Reassurance is another way. Children experience strong emotional needs — often without knowing why. Even without the rationale, though, the feelings are real. A calm look, an acceptance of emotionality, a recognition that "things" really are difficult can all help.

Finally, establish clear agreements and let the children be responsible for them. You will spend the first several lessons establishing ground rules with the children. These provide freedom and clear limits. In that process, return power to the group — look for consensus.

Managing Group Dynamics and Discipline Alternatives

TECHNIQUES TO FOCUS ON BEHAVIORS

What are you doing right now? This is asking the students to observe their own behavior, and in the observing to come to the conclusion that there might be another way to behave.

Be Somebody Else. Whenever there is a conflict or difference of opinion in the class so emotional or involving that the participants find it hard to be rational, ask them to imagine ("See in your head." "Hear in your head.") being the other person. Ask yourself the question (as the other person), "What do I need right now?" If the arguers can, have them take the role of the other person. See if they can see themselves and the situation from the other side.

Freeze. This is a stronger version of, "What are you doing now?" for any kind of intense group behavior. You call out, "Freeze!" Insist that everyone stop and stay frozen in position. Then direct the children to observe themselves, asking them to think about what was happening. When you say, "Unfreeze," generally the group will be calmer and willing to reflect.

Labeling the Behavior as Unacceptable. Sometimes just your labeling a specific behavior is enough to deal with the behavior. As with any other kind of labeling, name the specific behavior; avoid generalizing. If the disruptive behavior continues, ask for group consensus on how to handle it. Begin negotiation by using **your** own feelings (e.g., "Sam, I feel like you have interrupted me three times, and it makes me feel like you don't respect my feelings. Can the group help us solve this?")

EXERCISES TO BLOW OFF STEAM

Sometimes the energy level of the group is so high, trying to work against it is counterproductive. Energy-reducing activities help clear the air. They also serve the purpose of helping students become more aware of their feelings, and as such, are used formally in some of the lessons. Two example are:

Silent Screams. Sit, stand, or look in a mirror. Ask the students to scream as loud as they can scream **without sound**... scream with a whisper... scream with their bodies... scream like their teacher... scream because they are mad, excited, scared, happy... scream silently... scream like a mouse... scream in the littlest voice you have.

Explode. This is a tag game. You or an appointed leader are "It." Whomever the leader tags must "explode!" (i.e., scream, jump, fall, growl, whatever; to the degree the student wants to ventilate feelings).

Use these techniques as the situation seems to demand. By accepting the premise that a great deal of learning goes on through these techniques, you may feel less frustrated if a planned lesson gets interrupted. You don't have to "go" with the group feeling at all times. Sometimes **ignoring** it will help it to pass as well.

Self-Science Evaluation Form

FOR ALL TEACHERS TO DESCRIBE THE EFFECTS OF SELF-SCIENCE:

1. What have you observed to be the effect of Self-Science upon your students? (Where possible, give specific examples of the effect on particular children. Do not use their names.)

2. In addition to whatever effect Self-Science has had on the students' social and emotional development, has there been any effect in academic areas? Do they seem to apply any of the Self-Science techniques to academic subjects and/or extra curricular activities?

3. Have you incorporated Self-Science concepts in your work? If so, how? With what effect? What problems, if any, have you encountered in doing so? If not, why not?

4. Do you think Self-Science should be a part of the regular curriculum? If so, how should this be done? How should teachers be prepared?

Signed _____

From Self-Science, McCown, Jensen et al. ©1998, Six Seconds. The owner of this book has permission to copy this page.

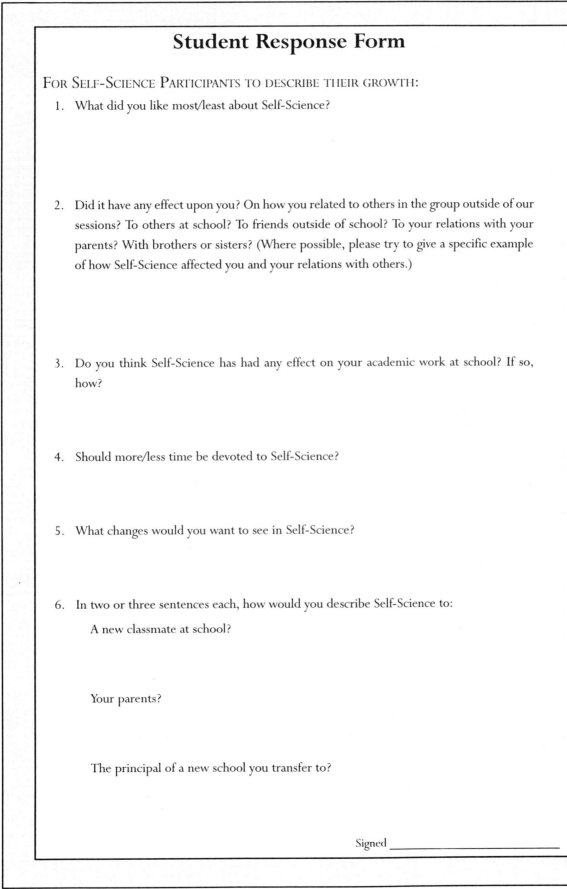

Student Response Form

FOR SELF-SCIENCE PARTICIPANTS TO DESCRIBE THEIR GROWTH:

1. What did you like most/least about Self-Science?

2. Did it have any effect upon you? On how you related to others in the group outside of our sessions? To others at school? To friends outside of school? To your relations with your parents? With brothers or sisters? (Where possible, please try to give a specific example of how Self-Science affected you and your relations with others.)

3. Do you think Self-Science has had any effect on your academic work at school? If so, how?

4. Should more/less time be devoted to Self-Science?

5. What changes would you want to see in Self-Science?

6. In two or three sentences each, how would you describe Self-Science to:

    A new classmate at school?

    Your parents?

    The principal of a new school you transfer to?

    Signed _____

From Self-Science, McCown, Jensen et al. ©1998, Six Seconds. The owner of this book has permission to copy this page.

Parent Response Form

FOR PARENTS OF CHILDREN PARTICIPATING IN SELF-SCIENCE:

As you know, your son/daughter has been participating in our Self-Science program. We are interested in its effect on children and would appreciate your taking the time to answer the following questions. We find that anonymous feedback is less valuable, so we would prefer that you sign your form. We will not use names, however, in any report about the program.

Thank you!

1. Has your child discussed Self-Science with you? What has s/he said about it? What it is? What we do in Self-Science? How does s/he feel about it?

2. Have you noticed any changes in your child's behavior since s/he has been participating in Self-Science? In how s/he relates to friends? Siblings? You? Please be as specific as possible.

3. If you have child(ren) who is (are) not in Self-Science, do you notice any difference in how they deal with their emotions and/or relate to other people?

4. Has Self-Science had any effect on your child's academic work?

5. Do you think Self-Science is a valuable part of the curriculum? Would you want to see it expanded or reduced? If you have children at other schools, would Self-Science be valuable there?

Signed _____

From Self-Science, McCown, Jensen et al. ©1998, Six Seconds. The owner of this book has permission to copy this page.

Figure 15: Rubric for EQ Assessment

From Self-Science, McCown, Jensen et al. ©1998, Six Seconds. The owner of this book has permission to copy this page.

EQ (emotional intelligence) Behaviors	Example of emerging level behavior	Example of sophisticated level behavior	Example of this person's behavior in this area	Demonstrated frequency of behavior Consistent ... Frequent ... Intermittent ... Rare
Demonstrates empathy	Comforting touch or pat to person who is distressed.	Accommodates frustrating behaviors from distressed friend.		
Communicates own feelings	Labels core emotions (e.g., I am happy).	Labels blends of emotions, (e.g., I am frustrated but hopeful).		
Controls impulsive behavior	Sort-term delay of gratification (e.g., saves candy for later).	Redirects impulse, (e.g., goes jogging when frustrated).		
Sets and works toward goals	Plans cause and effect, (e.g., I will read three pages before I break).	Manages multi-step process over months.		
Takes care of own emotional needs	Chooses friends who treat her well.	Validates own good behavior & principles.		
Listens to / focuses attention on others	Is quiet when someone else tells a story.	Reinforces listening through body language and sounds.		
Includes and reaches out to others	Acknowledges presence of others even when otherwise engaged.	Sits with people who are not friends or popular.		
Respects group	Uses kind/healing/nice words.	Volunteers to tutor others in free time.		
Accountable for behavior	Admits to tearing a book.	Voluntarily tells teacher it was not fair that he got extra time on paper.		
Uses optimism	Tomorrow I will try the big slide again.	I failed because I did not study enough but I m not a failure.		

The ability to actualize these behaviors varies greatly with development and environment.

1998, Six Seconds (650) 685-9885

Appendix E: Open Agenda Student Initiated Session (OASIS) Topics

OASIS are unstructured times for students to define the agenda. Though the subject matter is open, the process of Self-Science is reinforced and the same processes and ground rules should be used. Ideally, OASIS should be scheduled at least once per month.

Planned lessons usually include some OASIS time or at least some of the same qualities, simply because the group spirit that day will demand dealing with the children's concerns. In this case, it's usually better to go with the group, dealing with whatever evoked the concern, and come back to the lesson plan the next time. As you become more familiar with the goals of the curriculum and the Trumpet process, you will use OASIS more frequently. These non-structured sessions, initiated by students, create buy-in and indicate an openness and trust that allows them to deal with personal concerns.

SUGGESTED TOPICS

Undoubtedly, your own group will provide a wealth of topics for OASIS . There are also topics that most groups bring forth:

Just plain talking	Birthdays	Sex
Adoption	Holidays	Siblings
Friends	What happened during vacation	Illness
Homework	Divorce	Death

NOTES FROM KAREN'S JOURNAL

Birthdays

It was Jon's birthday, so we did The Birthday Experiment. The children love to talk about their birthdays. We had a brief discussion about why birthdays are important ("my own special day," "a celebration of me") and what they like most about birthdays. We described our favorite birthdays, birthday cakes, the earliest birthday we could remember, and the worst/best presents. We discussed how some people don't celebrate birthdays. Then we talked about the perfect birthday—when it would be, who'd be there, what we'd do, etc. Jon, Sue, Liz, Mark and Kelly all started giggling because even though they are 12, they like getting stuffed animals. The group ended up talking about why it is comforting to play with "kids" toys.

Appreciations

We opened by talking about Thanksgiving. They were thankful for friends, parents and for not having school, homework, etc. They told about Pilgrims, the Mayflower, the Indians and the Thanksgiving feast.

We suggested that we might make family appreciation cards for Thanksgiving and introduced "Appreciates." We had the children make a place card for each member of their family and write one thing they appreciate about that person on the card.

Mark made cards this time for his mother and father. Paul didn't want to make any. While we were doing this, we talked about what we would be doing for Thanksgiving. We all agreed it was a special time to be with our families.

They took the cards home to place on the table. Next time, we'll talk about how their families reacted.

Liz wanted to make cards for the group, so we did "appreciates," and everyone wrote a card for every other person.

Notes from Karen's Journal

Sex

It was mid-way through the year; this was a group of 11 and 12 year old students. The occasion was Valentine's Day. We asked the children what the meaning of Valentine's Day was, whereupon we heard a great deal of snickers and giggles from the students. With some continued prodding from the leaders, it became quite evident that their giggles were related to the topic of sex. No one, however, referred to it. "Well, you know what we're talking about; you know what it is." But no one was willing to talk about it.

As leaders, we decided that silently, all together, we would all whisper the word "sex." Then we all — leaders and students — said it softly, loudly, lowly, then quickly, until we were able to say the word without too much embarrassment.

We asked them if there were things that they wanted to know about sex. They all indicated that there were some things—but that they knew almost everything. By their demeanor, it was quite apparent that they were embarrassed to ask the question they wanted to for fear of appearing unknowledgeable in the area. Consequently we used the technique of having everybody write down a question about sex on a piece of paper. The questions were mixed in a container, passed out, and read anonymously. The total group participated in answering the questions.

Although there was some nervous laughter, most of the children—in fact, I believe all of the children—expressed relief in being able to frankly ask the questions that were of concern to them. The discussion of sex continued often after that, relating to such topics as kissing, masturbation, dating, etc. We encouraged the students to discuss these topics with their parents in order that family values/principles could be reinforced.

Adoption

Jill started talking about her birth certificate that said she was Norwegian and German, but that they could put anything they wanted on a birth certificate. Her sister, Alice, was a combination of lots of things. She thought it was better to just be from two nationalities. I asked why hers was different from her sister's, and she told everyone she was adopted. I asked Jill if she would like to talk about how it felt to be adopted. She said, "Yes." It didn't bother her a bit (very defensively). Terry said he used to think he was adopted because his older brother used to tell him he was when he was mad at him. Art and Doris said they'd thought about it sometimes, and I told Jill that I used to think I was adopted when I thought my mother was mean to me. Terry said he thought Jill didn't want to talk about being adopted, but she insisted that she did. I suggested that we talk about this after winter vacation. I felt Jill had revealed as much as she was comfortable with at the time. I suggested that we talk about our favorite holiday traditions and gifts.

NOTES FROM KAREN'S JOURNAL

Holidays

I mentioned that everyone in school seemed very excited, and several children shared that it was because the holdiay was coming soon. I asked everyone, "What is your favorite holiday?"

> "This year because I'm getting a large box that might be a drum set."
>
> "Last year because I got a bow and arrow."
>
> "Next year because I don't know what I'll get."
>
> "This year because I found some presents and I think they're for me."
>
> "This year because my grandmother is going to get me a Spanish doll."
>
> "When I got a Raggedy-Ann."
>
> "Last year, I got a bike."
>
> "Every Christmas."
>
> "This year because I got a desk with a locked drawer."
>
> "I never had Christmas. We have Hanukkah. I like every Hanukkah."
>
> "Can't decide. Last Christmas I went to my friend's house on Christmas Eve and this Christmas, we're going to Jamaica."
>
> "Last Christmas. I got a spinning wheel."

We talked about what we did over the winter holidays and about some of the customs we had in our families.

> "We have a tree and decorate it."
>
> "We open our presents on Christmas Day."
>
> "Some people open one on Christmas Eve."
>
> "Read *The Night Before Christmas*."
>
> "We light one candle each night."
>
> "Have to wait until everyone's awake."
>
> "At some houses, they decorate the tree on Christmas Eve."
>
> "We have special foods and feasts."
>
> "Hunt for presents that are hidden on Christmas Eve."
>
> Jack had a pattern of sneaking candy out of his sister's stocking.

We asked if there ever is a time when the holiday isn't fun.

> "Don't get what you want. You get disappointed."

The children asked to play Explode. (We were talking about unhappy holidays.)

> "Why do you need to explode?"
>
> "Need to waste energy. We have too much." "Because we're always inside." "Because I don't get to go outside." "Because we saw a ballet yesterday and we had to sit around a lot." "Because I like to run."

How do holidays make you feel?

> "Happy;" "good;" "makes you sad when it's over because you have to wait another year to get more presents."

Mary reminded us that we said we'd do the Video Camera Experiment today. The Speaker told what holiday presents s/he wanted.

> "All my wishes to come true; a GI Joe; helicopter; electric football; machine gun; tape recorder."
>
> "Puppy; watch; camera."
>
> "Puppy; watch."

Mark said his favorite present was a stuffed Teddy Bear that he had wanted for months. As a matter of fact, he still had it. He had about three stuffed animals. Billy was laughing. Mary turned to him and said, "What are you laughing about? There's nothing wrong with having stuffed animals." Billy said, "I know, I have some."

For the next half hour everyone in the group had a wonderful time reminiscing about being a little child. Sean told about the blanket he'd had since he was a baby. It had so many holes in it, it was a rag. When he was six he "acted like a big man," and told his mother he didn't want it any more and she could throw it away any time. About a week later he came home from school and ran all over the house looking for his blanket because he needed it. He finally asked his mother if she knew where it was. She had thrown it away He ran up to his room and cried because he still needed it, and it was gone.

Billy said he didn't have a blanket but he had a rubber Snoopy dog. He used to chew on the dog's nose instead of sucking his thumb or a pacifier. He recalled that he went through a number of Snoopies.

Jack told about his stuffed animals. He has a lot of them and one day he decided to give them a bath and they were ruined. He had a stuffed kitten with real fur and all the fur fell off and he felt really bad.

Mark remembered that he'd always wanted a little plastic lawn mower and he was so excited when he got one. All the boys had wanted this particular toy and they had great fun laughing together and remembering the lawns they pretended to be mowing. Mark also liked the GI Joe that he'd gotten even though the foot and hand fell off. At this point they all had a very lively discussion about GI Joe dolls, all of their equipment, how hard it was to dress them, all the imaginary games they played with them, and general relief that they all enjoyed this, including Sue who played with her brother's toys.

Sue recalled some dolls she had that she liked very much, but she talked a great deal with the boys about playing with toy soldiers and GI Joe men.

The entire group was very close today and really enjoyed reminiscing about earlier holiday seasons and being little children. We all wished each other happy holidays.

Notes from Karen's Journal

Illness

We had an interesting session talking about illness—our own and our parents'. Everyone told about their parents being ill and as they did, we asked them to show how they felt.

Dane said his mother was sick for three months and he stayed with his father. He saw her once a week and that helped, but he was lonesome for her and worried. He would have been worried to death if he hadn't been able to see her.

Tom said when he was six he was in the hospital with hepatitis. He was very ill and doesn't remember a lot. His father also had hepatitis and was in the hospital for three months. We asked him if he had worried about his father, but he said he was too sick himself to be aware that his father was sick.

Alan told about his mother having surgery a few years ago. He said he wasn't sure what it was, but he was scared when she was gone and she didn't feel well when she came home.

Sean told about his mother and father. His mother had to have her thyroid out and that was very serious because your thyroid gives you energy. She takes medicine every day. His father has an old back injury and he recently hurt it. Now he can hardly get around. Sean was very worried when his mother was sick and he felt sorry for his dad, but he knew he would get better.

I told about my mother being very sick in the hospital. I couldn't see her but my father took me to her window and I could look in. There were bars on the window. Everyone joined in the discussion on why there were bars. I told them maybe because the rooms on the first floor face a large open area and the bars are to keep people out.

Bob said it seemed like his mother was sick a very long time, although it was only ten days, and that he was scared because he couldn't see her.

Kelly told about her father's operation and how they sneaked into the hospital to see him. It worries her when her parents are sick.

Karen told about her mother who went to New York for three months to have an operation while her grandmother took care of her and her sister. She was very scared because her mother was gone so long and she was so far away.

We asked them what they worried about and they replied, ... they wouldn't get better; who'd take care of them? What would happen? We asked if they ever worried about their parents dying and they all said they had. After a brief discussion someone asked to play Explode.

Death

The group asked questions about Jon's absence. I explained that he had gone to Southern California to attend his grandfather's funeral. The group appeared very curious about the death and wanted to discuss the details of when his grandfather had died, how, where, and when the funeral was going to be. I said that I knew few details, but that Jon's grandfather was quite elderly. We proceeded to discuss how Jon might be feeling. Del and Kelly suggested that he might be feeling very sad. Billy and Kay suggested that he might feel relieved if his grandfather had been very old and sick. I asked if they had ever had anyone in their family or someone they know die. Several children in the group had experiences to share.

Terry, who has never offered to talk in the group before, told about his grandmother. "Before she died she was sick for a long time. She was little and very skinny and when you sat down next to her you had to be careful because it hurt her to be jarred. She was very old when she died and we all felt really sad." His tone of voice and demeanor appeared serious and he seemed to be re-experiencing some of the sadness in relation to his grandmother's death.

Art said, "When my grandmother died, we all felt really bad. She lived in Iowa and when we went to visit my grandfather in the summer we were all lonesome for my grandmother."

Del, "My uncle died and everyone felt really bad."

Kristi said, "We had a neighbor who had a seven year old daughter who was dying of cancer. She had seven operations before she died and she was very sick and weak. Everyone felt bad when she died but they were also relieved because she had suffered for so long. It was better that she died.

I really felt sad when our dog died. He was my best friend and he had been with our family ever since I was a baby. We grew up together and when he died I cried for a week and I felt like running away from home." She went on to explain how angry she was with her parents because they had to put the dog to sleep.

Jim interrupted and said he could never feel that bad about an animal dying—then he quietly said, "I know how it will feel when my mother dies."

Everyone in the room turned to look at him. The group had obviously heard Jim's comment and was somewhat shaken by it. Billy asked him how he knew that. He said,

NOTES FROM KAREN'S JOURNAL, CONT.

"When my mother went to India it was the saddest day of my life. I didn't think I could stand it—I cried for a week and I never felt so lonely and sad." The other group members wanted to know why his mother had gone to India, how long she would be there, where his father was, did he have any brothers or sisters, where were they, and how long would his parents be gone.

Jim, with sadness apparent in his voice and body movement, told how his parents were missionaries for the church. His father had been in India for one-and-one-half years before his mother left a year ago. They decided not to take him with them because the schools he would go to would be very bad. The only decent schools were English and they hit you with canes; he appeared to be trying to deal with his sense of loss by rationalizing about the schools. Jim went on to say he has one brother who is older than he is and is staying in Denver. He hadn't seen him since June, but was really looking forward to seeing him at Christmas. He told Jill, who talks a lot about how she dislikes her sister, that she wouldn't feel that way if she couldn't be with her sister. He used to fight a lot with his brother, but now he really missed him and knew how much he loved him. Jim's parents will be gone for one more year and when they come home they are going to have a huge bottle of champagne and a soufflé. Everyone in the group was moved by Jim's deep feelings for his family. He had tears in his eyes, as did several other children. There was a short silence as the group members appeared to be absorbing what Jim had been saying. Consequently at this point, it seemed appropriate for the group to review the major feelings of the discussion. I asked the group if they could recall all the different words we had used to describe our feelings about death. We remembered sad, lonely bad, unhappy, and relieved.

I then asked what happens when someone dies and Alan immediately said, "They leave you. They leave you forever." Again the whole group looked at Jim and everyone sat silently for a minute. Jim said in a very soft and saddened voice, "That was it. It was like she died because she went to India and left me and it seemed like forever." There were tears in everyone's eyes.

Alan, Billy and Kay all told about the times their parents had left them to go

on trips and how it had seemed like forever. I asked Alan if he resented his parents at all when they returned from a month in Europe. He said, "No," but then added, "Maybe a little. I was mad at them the next day." I suggested that it was very natural to feel some resentment towards people who leave us, even if they die. Alan said he remembered when he visited his grandfather after his grandmother died and he felt bad that she wasn't there to bake him his favorite cookies he always had before.

At this point, Jim said he felt like he needed to play Explode. Everyone agreed and immediately got up to play. Explode is like a game of tag. I am "It," and when I tag them, they are supposed to explode. We had played this game many times but no one had ever really exploded. There were a few yells, jumping onto the bean bag chairs but no explosion (i.e., real evidence of emotional release).

I tagged Jim first and he ran across the room and dove on a pile of bean bags yelling as loud as he could. Everyone froze for a minute to watch. He was face down, kicking his feet, pounding his fists, yelling. As I tagged each child he or she really exploded for the first time. When all had been tagged, they all wanted to play again. We played two more times. Each time the explosions were greater in intensity. After the third game, I suggested we all sit down quietly for a few minutes. We did some deep breathing exercises to get centered before leaving. The whole group seemed relaxed; before leaving, Jim quietly stated that he was glad he'd talked about his mother and he felt better.

Glossary

approach getting close to—movement towards a goal.

attending paying attention to, listening.

avoidance to withdraw—to keep away.

body talk using parts of the body to communicate nonverbally.

brainstorm a group problem solving technique that involves the spontaneous contribution of ideas from all members of the group.

centered to be in control of oneself.

censor withholding or keeping from the group information, thoughts or feelings.

concentric having a common center.

confidentiality private information that all agree not to share outside the group.

confrontation to face, to encounter—to bring out into the open.

consensus unanimous group agreement.

consequences the result of one's thoughts, feelings or actions.

continuum a chart or scale that measures from one extreme to another.

coping to deal with and/or attempt to overcome problems and difficulties.

deliberate careful, thorough consideration—awareness of consequences.

EQ emotional intelligence; abbreviation for "emotional quotient."

explicit statement clear, direct, non-ambiguous communication.

exploding to let go—to burst out with feelings.

fantasy the process of creating mental images (imagination).

inference moving from one proposition, statement or idea considered true, to another whose truth is believed to follow from the former.

inquiry to ask about—to seek information by questioning.

intimate a very close association—a warm friendship.

introspection examination of one's own thoughts and/or feelings.

killer statement a negative statement—an insult.

legitimize to affirm.

metaphor a comparison of two different objects or ideas that are alike in some essential manner.

modeling to serve as a pattern—an example for imitation or emulation.

nonverbal communication expressing one's self with little or no language.

pattern a repeated set of thoughts, feelings or actions that characterize an individual.

power control, authority or influence over self and/or others.

projection to describe, make statements or judgments about another that are true of one's self.

re-own to take back for oneself descriptions, statements or judgments one has made about an object or person.

resents a statement of what one does not like.

role-play to act out/pretend to be someone or something else.

self disclosure to open up—to talk about one's self.

self-esteem positive self-concept or understanding of self.

Self-Science studying self using the scientific process.

values something (a principle or quality or belief) attributed to be desirably worthwhile, important, good, evil, etc.

We Need Your Comments

Your comments, questions, and ideas will shape future editions of this curriculum. We are committed to creating a curriculum that meets teachers' needs. In fact, if we use an idea, story, or lesson you send, we will pay you for your contribution. So email, fax, or write us today.

Six Seconds
316 Seville Way
San Mateo, CA 94402
(650) 685-9885
(650) 685-9880 - fax
staff@6seconds.org

6seconds

A nonprofit educational service organization providing
training and materials for emotional intelliegence.

Training for schools, communities, families and
corporations:

Teaching EQ

Making Conflict Positive

Communication

Principle Based Behavior

Motivation

Goal Setting

Six Seconds

316 Seville Way

San Mateo, CA 94402

(650) 685-9885

(650) 685-9880 - fax

staff@6seconds.org

Six Seconds is a 501(c)3 charitable organization.

Create a culture of respect, responsibility and resiliency.

www.6seconds.org

Handle With Care Activity Book

24 themes of emotional intelligence explored through activities, quotes, role models, books, movies and thought-provoking questions.

The Activity Book includes an invaluable introduction to emotional intelligence and strategies to teach these critical skills. It also includes over 175 full color stickers and 12 postcards.

If you appreciate the *Handle With Care* calendar, you'll love this book! A "must-have" for anyone concerned about children and emotional intelligence.

112 pages, softcover, $16.95. Call (650) 685-9885 to reserve your copy now! Shipping June 25, 1998.

Interdependence Quotes

"We have committed the Golden Rule to memory; let us now commit it to life."
— Edwin Markham

"Do not wait for leaders; do it alone, person to person."
— Mother Teresa

"Power is the ability to do good things for others."
— Brooke Astor

"Man does not weave this web of life. He is merely a strand of it. Whatever he does to the web, he d   to himself."
— Chie

Interdependence Questions

Do you gain freedom or loose freedom by accepting interdependenc

In the picture below, you can see a buffalo (it is "Yellowstone Christm   August 25, 1989). How does this photo show interdependence?

Can you create interdependence with someone who wants to be inde   dent from you?

If you were making an illustration for interdependence, what image would you use? What would you want to make people feel?

Which is more interdependent, a circle or a square?

Motivation Activities

• Pick something you have always wanted to do — learning a skill, playing an instrument, creating a project — schedule the time, and do it!

• When a child or friend comes to you with a problem, don't fix it (this is hard! Be strict with yourself). Instead, support her and help her understand the problem. Offer her support to generate her own solution.

• Make sure your child has real choice about important matters in the family. Make sure there are areas of children's lives in which they have total control. Also, ensure that child input is a part of the family decision-making process.

• Spontaneous and unexpected rewards build internal motivation. When someone you love does something well, have a special celebration, buy a popsicle, put up streamers, throw confetti.

• Negotiated incentives and consequences are effective when they are consistent and when both (or all) parties agree. Create a reward system for yourself, your family or your workplace. There can be many stages of reward from "if we are on time all day we'll have ice cream" to "if we get this project done on time, everybody gets three days off." The overlapping combination of short term and long term, big and small, is most effective.

• Pick three activities you love to do and list the reasons you are motivated for that; can you use those motivations someplace else?

"If you won't be better tomorrow than you were today, then what do you need tomorrow for?"

Includes a plethora of EQ stickers for fun and learning.

Empathy

Emotional Intelligence
Adversity
Interdependence
Creativity
Motivation
Accountability
Forgiveness
Conflict
Tolerance
Truth
Awareness
Self Control
Integrity